ICONIC
New York
JEWISH FOOD

A HISTORY AND GUIDE
WITH RECIPES

JUNE HERSH

AMERICAN PALATE

Published by American Palate
A Division of The History Press
Charleston, SC
www.historypress.com

First published 2023

Manufactured in the United States

ISBN 9781467152600

Library of Congress Control Number: 2022947154

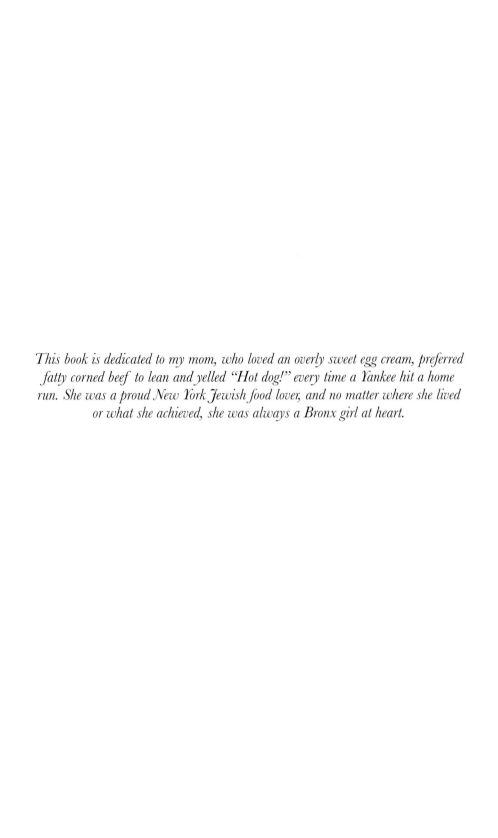

This book is dedicated to my mom, who loved an overly sweet egg cream, preferred fatty corned beef to lean and yelled "Hot dog!" every time a Yankee hit a home run. She was a proud New York Jewish food lover, and no matter where she lived or what she achieved, she was always a Bronx girl at heart.

CONTENTS

FOREWORD

We are very pleased to be partnering with June Hersh on this culinary journey that celebrates the history and longevity of New York's iconic Jewish food. The foods presented in this text might have derived from immigrant foodways, but they have been embraced by people of all backgrounds. As an organization founded more than fifty years ago on the Jewish values of integrity, compassion and respect, we, too, embrace and serve everyone, regardless of race, ethnicity or religion. Met Council operates the largest emergency food system in America, focused on helping individuals and families who maintain kosher diets, as well as other religiously informed dietary practices. Its mission is to provide a dignified solution to hunger. Through a comprehensive array of food programs and social services funded by the support of readers like you and agencies such as UJA-Federation, we administer immediate assistance and help to create pathways to self-sufficiency for more than 315,000 clients each year. In a city where there is a bagel shop in every neighborhood, there are neighbors who are struggling with food insecurity. It is our goal to alleviate this issue and make New York City not only the food capital of the world but also a place where no one goes hungry. We hope that this book will engage, enlighten and enrich your New York City food experience, while helping to support those in need. To quote June, it is a way to "Eat Well—Do Good." Learn more at metcouncil.org.

DAVID GREENFIELD,
Chief Executive Officer, Met Council

ACKNOWLEDGEMENTS

*W*hen I wrote my first book, *Recipes Remembered: A Celebration of Survival,* I had the distinct honor of meeting and developing relationships with a remarkable community of Holocaust survivors. They imbued me with a perspective on my life that has forever changed me. For this book, I was not able to meet most of the people I was writing about. Without the advantage of a time machine, I was unable to hear their energized voices or ask them how they accomplished all that they did. But their legacy was very clear. A group of hopeful immigrants set sail for a new life in a new place and not only made it their home but also made it an infinitely more delicious and diverse place to live. They brought their foodways to New York and developed foods, products and businesses that endure today. So, my first thank-you is to that brave group, those people who sought a better life, asked for little and contributed so much. That immigrant spirit continues today and makes New York a more delicious destination.

I would not be a food writer today were it not for the lessons and encouragement of Andrew F. Smith, my literary guardian angel. I thank him for all that I have endeavored to do in the pursuit of chronicling and documenting food history. My family is also integral to my process. They listen as I read and re-read a paragraph that sounds remarkably the same and are challenged to find the one word I am obsessing over. They hear more than once the stories I find fascinating and taste every recipe I test. I devour their enthusiasm for what I am doing and thank them for their love and support.

This work would not have been possible without input from many people involved in the New York food scene. From bagel makers and smokehouse owners to the deli man behind the counter who speared my slab of pastrami over and over again so I could take the perfect picture. I thank them for continuing the wonderful traditions started more than a century ago and showing respect for the food that is now iconic to the New York food landscape. A special shout-out to the experts I spoke with, especially the team at Mt. Kisco Bagels, the team at Mt. Kisco Smokehouse, Mike Varley of Highley Varlet, Emily and Adam Caslow, Ellen Lee-Allen of Acme Smoked Fish Corporation, Michelle Young at Untapped NY, Aliza Gans of Russ & Daughters, Gary Greengrass of Barney Greengrass, Peter Shelsky of Shelsky's, Riyadh Gazali of David's Brisket House, the team at Katz's Deli, Lana Dubin from the Tenement Museum, Andrew Leibowitz of Guss' Pickles, Alan Kaufman of the Pickle Guys, Burt Rapoport, the team at Yonah Schimmel's, John Philis of Lexington Candy Shop, Alex Gomberg of Brooklyn Seltzer Boys, Herb Glaser, Stuart and Michael Zaro, Ben Green of Green's Bakery, Kristina Beauchamp and Alan Rosen of Junior's and Mitchell and Skye Cohen of Economy Candy. I am so pleased to be able to thank Senior Director of Development and Donor Relations Amy Gazley and Chief Executive Officer David Greenfield of Met Council for for facilitating our partnership and writing such a meaningful preface. Thank you to my "A team" of chefs and authors Jake Cohen, Silvia Baldini, Suzanne Gold, Ellie Krieger and Jeffrey Yoskowitz for their gracious contribution and support.

It is almost cliché to say (but isn't that how it becomes cliché?) that there would be no book without the commitment and vision of the team at The History Press. Thank you to J. Banks Smither, my acquisitions editor, who saw merit in this book and encouraged me to pursue every tangential path that led me to something interesting and delicious. His tireless input and enthusiasm made this process fun and exciting. I do believe that somewhere in that amazing Charleston exterior he is also a nice Jewish boy at heart! Thank you to Senior Editor Ryan Finn, who made sure that every *i* was dotted and *t* crossed and that my voice remained my own while making the book clear and precise. Many thanks to Caroline Rodrigues, who helped format the images so they met specs for publication, and Anna Renninger Burrous, who beautifully designed the cover.

Lastly, I thank you, the reader, for your time and attention to the stories and foods presented in this book. While they might represent the food brought to New York by one culture, it speaks volumes to the spirit of New York in embracing them. This is a city built on acceptance; it has always been flavored with so many forms of cultural expression, and I am hoping that we continue to celebrate the many aspects of the city that make it so much more than the sum of its parts.

INTRODUCTION

*E*very food has a story and every dish a language. San Francisco's cioppino can be traced to the arrival of Italian fishermen, and it speaks with a Genoese flair. Jambalaya is imbedded in French Huguenot influences and talks with a Cajun twist. So, it should be no surprise that the iconic foods of New York have rich historical context and a language intertwined with its ancestry. What is revelatory is how many of the foods associated with New York City find their lineage in eastern Europe and their voice imbued with a Yiddish accent. New York City is the home to immigrants from all over the world, and its food is as rich and flavorful as the people who inhabit it. As a proud New Yorker, born in the Bronx and raised in the burbs who enjoys everything New York City has to offer, I can say with conviction and a touch of bias that it is the undeniable food capital of the world. People flock to the city from all over the globe to taste our iconic food, and New Yorkers continue to devour these dishes more than a century after they were first introduced.

Labeling the foods and establishments in this book as iconic is a brash and bold statement. Iconic status is reserved for legends in theater, art, literature and music. It implies that there is no equal and that its classic status is unquestionable and enduring. But how do you judge when one person's food obsession could be another's overrated taste sensation? Sometimes the emperor is resplendent and sometimes he has no clothes, so achieving this distinction could be a matter of individual taste. Therefore, to call a food iconic you need objective rather than subjective measures. It must be instantly recognizable and survive menu changes and a pandemic. It must have a fascinating past, a solid place in the present and an unlimited future. It should

David expounds the Melting Pot to Vera—Act I.

A scene from Israel Zangwill's play *The Melting Pot*, as performed in 1909 at the Billy Rose Theatre. *NYPL Billy Rose Theatre Collection.*

warrant long waits on endless lines and frequent mentions in pop culture. For restaurants, the bar is set differently. Iconic restaurants that are gone should leave diners hungry for nostalgia, and those that still exist should consistently replicate their magic day after day. As with the chicken and the egg, it is hard to know whether the foods elevated the restaurant or the restaurant elevated the food. This book celebrates the interconnected history of emblematic foods and institutions synonymous with New York.

Because this book is focused on those offerings in the New York food landscape, whose family tree is rooted in Jewish culture, the next imposing question is "What makes a food Jewish?" Culinary historians might argue that there is no such thing as a purely Jewish food other than matzo. There is no one country that Jewish people hail from or one cuisine that identifies that cooking style. Jewish food reflects a diaspora. The pot didn't just melt—it burst, mingling cultures, ingredients and techniques. I often say that Jews have been thrown out of all the best food countries on the planet and have taken their spiritual, physical and cultural journey, with those influences firmly imbedded in their collective cooking DNA. How do you trace the origins of a dish considered to be Jewish when the stories surrounding it are blurry and tend toward myth and legend rather than hard truth? How do you differentiate between a dish inherently Jewish in origin or one that Jewish people absorbed and transformed because of circumstance? And how do you define a cooking style that has to conform to standards set not by the FDA but by the Torah and Talmud, with ingredients that have rules?

I suggest that Jewish foods are those that have developed a Jewish profile because of the people and places that made them famous. The late Lenny Bruce once quipped, "Kool-Aid is goyish. Evaporated milk is goyish, even if the Jews invented it. Chocolate is Jewish and fudge is goyish....Pumpernickel is Jewish and, as you know, white bread is very goyish." There is no real reason for these associations, but they invariably and tenaciously exist—some foods just feel Jewish. Professor Jonathan Brumberg, whose life work is examining Jewish foodways, wrote in his book *Gastronomic Judaism as Culinary Midrash* that "Jewish foods are exercises in culinary improvisations, that is, efforts to take a variety of inherited Jewish food related principles and apply them to new and different food ingredients, situations, places and times." This explains the way the new immigrants adopted, adjusted and assimilated when they arrived in New York. They incorporated the food of their homeland into their new life, as a lifeline to their former one, and took the foods they found here and made them part of their new experience. Being a gastronomic Jew in New York at the turn of the century meant navigating how to incorporate religious aspects of Judaism into a seamless culinary experience based on your new surroundings, neighbors and resources.

You might question some of the inclusions, even I did. Are chop suey or Manischewitz wine iconic New York foods? The simple answer is no. Almost never does someone come specifically to New York to sample these products, and they probably wouldn't make the Top 20 list if you were asked to compile one. However, in researching this book, there were traditions and products that begged to be explored. To deprive you, the reader, of knowing why Jewish Americans celebrate Christmas at their local Chinese restaurant or why Sammy Davis Jr. became the spokesperson for Manischewitz wine would be a disservice to you and the topic, as they are imbedded with New York culture. So, if I digress at some points or follow a tangential lead that takes us a bit off path, I hope you know that I did it for you. You'll also find a recipe or two at the end of each chapter. They each relate to the theme of the chapter and are not newfangled or profound reinterpretations. No deconstructed knishes or jalapeño matzo balls here. These recipes are rooted in tradition, tested by time and easy to replicate in your home to bring an authentic experience to the table.

Let's put all these factors together. We present nibbles, noshes and nourishment that define the cuisine of a city and one inextricably linked to the Ashkenazi Jewish immigrant experience. The question beckons: Is this a book that highlights New York's iconic foods that happen to be Jewish…or Jewish iconic foods that were introduced and popularized in New York? The answer is yes. In writing the book, it was hard to separate where one ended and the other began. What I do know is that, quoting Lenny Bruce once more, "If you live in New York, you are Jewish. Even if you're Catholic, you are Jewish." To a great extent, he is correct. Whether by association or osmosis, there is a Jewishness that permeates the city. Ask any cabbie when Rosh Hashanah begins, and he can tell you the precise time. Order a bagel with a schmear of cream cheese from a bodega and no translation is needed. New Yorkers have embraced Jewish food, and Jewish food has transformed New Yorkers. Whether it migrates naturally as people move to

A 1902 image of immigrants arriving at Ellis Island. *Library of Congress, Prints and Photographs Division.*

a new place or is carried back as a vivid food memory by a smitten visitor, New York food in turn becomes American food. It's not just New Yorkers who feel that brunch without lox and bagels is just not brunch. As Claudia Roden, one of the most acclaimed voices in the world of Jewish food, noted, "The adoption of bagels as a national bread—and lox and bagels as the grandest American breakfast—and of cheesecake as the All-American cake symbolizes the integration of Jews in American life, and their part in shaping the ethos and character of the country and its largest city."

Perhaps most of all, this book recognizes the imprecise. Let's accept that some of the tales told are what can be called "underground history," more like a game of telephone rather than an answer on *Jeopardy*. Let's agree that I cannot cover every food or restaurant, trend or business, but I will try to review those that were most impactful. Let's not groan at the plethora of puns— when dealing with foods like pickles, it should be no big dill. Let's recognize that some of the foods or restaurants are not iconic on their own but are part of an experience that is. Let's acknowledge that some Yiddish and Jewish words have multiple spellings. Even the 86th Scripps National Spelling Bee created a controversy with the spelling of the winning word *kneidel* (Yiddish for dumpling, matzo ball). Most importantly, let's celebrate the amazing influence that a group of immigrants who arrived in New York with little more than small suitcases and lifetimes of tradition imprinted on the way New York City eats. And then let's delight in the fact that these same foods and establishments have become iconic as they are embraced across this country and the globe. These foods beckon tourists and feed the masses. These establishments set the tone for all that is replicated elsewhere. They represent a food tapestry woven with fibers that are not frayed, threadbare or showing any sign of age. They hold strong and continue to blanket us with comfort.

COMING TO AMERICA

Far, we've been traveling far
Without a home but not without a star
Free, only want to be free
We huddle close, hang on to a dream

JEWISH GEOGRAPHY

Long before Neil Diamond wrote these lyrics, immigrants were arriving on our shores with hopes for a better life. The push to leave came from economic strife, political upheaval and religious persecution. The pull to America was opportunity; having little to lose or leave behind, they sought the American dream. Every group of immigrants that has come to New York has imprinted its culture on ours. As groups flow in and settle neighborhoods, they infuse their personality and, in turn, the food with their own traditions, and New York is richer for having their influences. However, when they arrive in large numbers at a time, their impact is magnified. Such was the case with the waves of Jewish immigrants that arrived between 1820 and 1924.

The first Jewish immigrants to settle in New York came well before the two great waves. In 1654, twenty-three Sephardic Jews fled the Portuguese inquisition that overtook their home in Recife, Brazil. They settled in what was then New Amsterdam and became fully integrated into New York life. It's interesting to note that Emma Lazarus, who penned the immortal words that are inscribed on the base of the Statue of Liberty—"Give me your

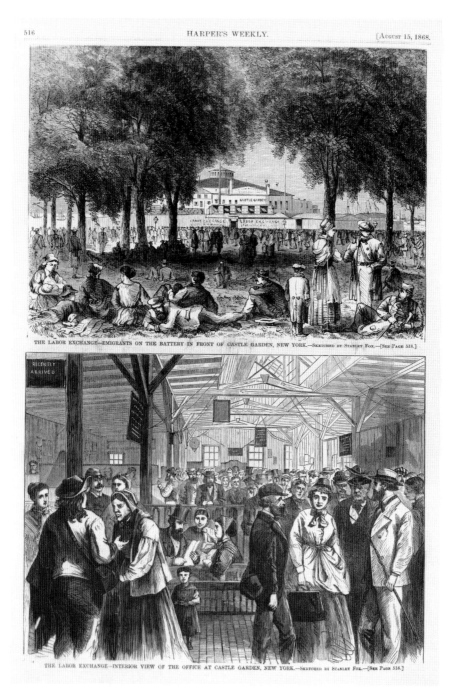

A sketch dating back to 1868 that appeared in *Harper's Weekly*, captioned, "Emigrants on the Battery in front of Castle Garden." *Library of Congress, Prints and Photographs Division.*

GERMAN IMMIGRANTS—THEIR ARRIVAL AT NEW-YORK.

Newly arriving well-dressed and sophisticated German immigrants. *NYPL, Miriam and Ira D. Wallach Division of Art, Prints and Photographs.*

tired your poor, your huddled masses yearning to breathe free"—was a descendant of those Sephardic Jews.

The first large influx were mainly Germans who were escaping economic hardship and restrictive laws that dictated their day-to-day activities. They arrived in the early to mid-1800s at Castle Garden, a receiving center at the southern tip of Manhattan that predated Ellis Island. These earliest German Jewish immigrants, according to Professor of Jewish Studies Michael Meyer, were peddlers and cattle dealers, and many settled in the Midwest, most notably Cincinnati. The immigrants were mostly men, who would send for their families once they established themselves in America, a phenomenon that today is termed "chain migration." Those who came a bit later after the German revolution of 1848 were more educated, urbane and sophisticated. With their arrival, New York's Jewish population increased tenfold, as did their influences on New York culture.

The period between 1880 and 1924 was filled with tremendous upheaval for eastern European Jews, especially those in Poland, Ukraine, Lithuania and Russia. These countries fell into what was known as the "Pale of Settlement," an area designated by Catherine II where Jews could reside. They were plagued by pogroms, persecution and poverty. The promise of prosperity was promoted throughout eastern Europe, with pamphlets and advertisements encouraging and inviting immigrants to come to America, and they did in droves. To grasp their impact, according to the course seminar "The Peopling of New York," presented by Brooklyn College, prior to their arrival in 1880 there were about sixty-thousand Jews in New York City. By 1914, it had swelled to 1.5 million, an increase of 2,500 percent. These immigrants, unlike the German wave, came as whole families. They were characterized as more religious, impoverished and less educated. They were slower to assimilate and in great numbers retained their adherence to dietary laws.

New York City is defined by bravado and boroughs, and each of the five boroughs of New York City was infused with immigrants and, in turn, their culture. Manhattan, which some unabashedly and immodestly simply call "the city," was the home to most of the earlier arrivals. But immigrants did live in other boroughs as well. Brooklyn saw its fair share, as did *the* Bronx (and yes, you need to include that important article). To a lesser extent, they gravitated to Queens, and a small number went to Staten Island. Jewish immigrants, like so many other newcomers, tended to self-ghettoize, creating ethnic enclaves. Jewish people did so especially on the Lower East Side (LES), where they crammed into an area that is a mere 536 acres, less than one square mile. Of the 2.5 million Jewish immigrants to arrive, close to 1 million settled on the Lower East Side, mainly in the tenth ward. This created the largest Jewish community anywhere and the most densely populated place on the planet. Their influence permeated every aspect of daily life, from the foods they enjoyed to the trades they supported. These immigrants brought with them those foods that we traditionally think of as being Jewish: matzo ball soup, chopped liver, smoked fish and bagels. They baked babkas and rugelach and stuffed kishkes and knishes. You could fall into a Jewish food coma by simply walking the neighborhood. They changed the culinary landscape and became the trailblazers for most of the iconic New York foods we enjoy today. Currently, the Lower East Side is home to a great mix of New Yorkers, which is reflected in the mashup of stores and restaurants lining the streets. From Japanese Omakase to Cuban cuisine, there is not an ethnicity or food style that is not represented on the LES. However, it is still home to many of the original Ashkenazi trailblazers.

While a large number of German Jews settled on the Lower East Side, many traveled uptown to an area known as Yorkville, on the Upper East Side (UES), which became a second *Kleindeutschland*, "Little Germany." Yorkville is only a half square mile, yet it became a center of ideological, cultural and Jewish culinary influences. These Jews are credited with establishing Mount Sinai Hospital and Temple Emanu-El, the largest Reform congregation in the United States. From a culinary standpoint, they excelled in baking, were masters of butchery and established the first delicatessens. While they didn't create pastrami or corned beef, they gave it a place to shine, and don't get me started as to what they did for the hot dog. Today, Yorkville is still dotted with some of the original shops, but back in the day they were ubiquitous. It was an upscale way to get your Ashkenazi Jewish food fix.

Section of lower Manhattan in 1899, showing Mulberry Bend Park (created on the site of Mulberry Bend in 1895 after Riis's disclosures), Chinatown, Five Points, Jewish neighborhoods on Bayard and Baxter Streets, and adjacent wards.

This 1890 map illustrates the area of the Lower East Side, as surveyed by Jacob Riis during his work on *How the Other Half Lives. authentichistory.com.*

The Lower and Upper East Sides were not the only neighborhoods in Manhattan that attracted Jewish immigrants. The Upper West Side (UWS), as well as Harlem to the extreme north, saw its fair share. The UWS became a hub of Jewish social and culinary activity as synagogues, organizations and restaurants featuring Jewish food flourished. After World War II, an area called Washington Heights, on the upper Upper West Side, became home to many Holocaust survivors and refugees from the war. They solidified the Jewish influences in cuisine in that northernmost part of Manhattan. The UWS still remains a heavily populated Jewish area, and the stores and establishments that began there and still exist today speak to the influence of that demographic.

Jerome Meyers sketched this charcoal drawing in 1912 showing Jewish immigrants in a piece he titled *Pushcarts and Immigrants*. *Metropolitan Museum of Art, Wikimedia Commons.*

Brooklyn was also a haven for immigrants and continues to be for the new waves coming from Israel, Russia and the Middle East. Their greatest mass migration was in the 1920s and 1930s, when a large number of Orthodox families left Manhattan and moved to Williamsburg and Borough Park, Crown Heights and Bedford-Stuyvesant (Bed-Stuy) in Brooklyn. The construction of bridges and railways to connect Brooklyn to Manhattan made the commute less arduous and the transplanting easier. By 1923, the numbers had shifted, and Brooklyn now had the largest Jewish population of any borough in the city. Brooklyn was the hub for smoked fish and cured and smoked meat, as well as pickles, hot dogs, candy and seltzer. After World War II, Brooklyn swelled when the Hasidic Jews immigrated to the United States and settled there. Yiddish became the language of choice once again in places such as Williamsburg and Brighton Beach, otherwise known as Little Odessa. Brooklyn is a true dichotomy, with very old-world Hasidic influences mixing with a "hipster" vibe. That's why it is no surprise that Brooklyn is the home to both kosher stores and restaurants as well as some of the new and innovative delis and appetizing stores that are revitalizing Jewish cuisine.

Let's not forget that there are three other boroughs where the immigrants settled, albeit in far fewer numbers. That could be why you won't find a concentration of Jewish-inspired food in these boroughs to the same extent. However, parts of the Bronx did boast a strong community, especially in the southern section. The boulevards in that area, such as the Grand Concourse, mimicked those on the UWS and were home to some of the more middle-class Jewish families. That is no longer the case, as those neighborhoods now enjoy a true mix of cultures and ethnicities, and the stores and restaurants reflect that change. Queens and Staten Island have always had fewer Jewish residents, and so you'll see fewer Jewish style stores in either of those boroughs.

Jewish geography is a game every Jewish family plays, as they tend to experience two rather than six degrees of separation. That was definitely the case during these great waves of immigration. Unlike other groups of immigrants who arrived during this period of time, Jewish immigrants stayed put. Nearly 30 percent of other groups returned to their original country, but more than 90 percent of Jewish immigrants planted roots. That speaks volumes as to the social and cultural effects they had long term on the neighborhoods where they settled.

It's hard to imagine that any of the new Americans who arrived during this great influx would envision the lasting impact their foodways would have on their neighborhood, the city as a whole and the country at large. Their acceptance into New York's culture and mainstream America is more far reaching than the bravado and boroughs that ignited them.

THE SIDEWALKS OF NEW YORK

Pushcarts and peddlers might conjure up the opening number from *Fiddler on the Roof*, but this accurately described the way of life for many immigrants who came to New York City. While they seem like iterations of the same profession, they were distinctive forms of commerce. Pushcarts could be either stationary stalls, or kiosks on wheels, that serviced a neighborhood. Peddlers were on foot, carrying as much as 150 pounds on their backs, delivering their products to homes and businesses. There was also a distinctive class of peddlers who traveled to far-flung areas of the country, staying away from home at long stretches of time. These itinerant peddlers brought food customs to the communities they visited and brought some regional customs back home. Professor Michael A. Meyer in a lecture at Indiana University referenced a peddler who kept a diary. This immigrant wrote in his broken German/English, "As matters stand here, I'm buried alive. I have to peddle and ask, 'Do you want to buy,' and sweat and carry my basket!" Such was the difficult life of the Jewish peddler on the American frontier.

With the tremendous influx of immigrants, the lure of familiarity created marketplaces that featured anything you could imagine. Nearly every culture had vendors selling everything from Italian salami to Greek olives. Jewish vendors offered practical products like prayer books and shawls, as well as comfort food like herring and pickles. While these immigrants longed to belong, they were nostalgic for the foods that made their new home feel reminiscent of their old one. Food writer John Mariani wrote that the lure of America were streets paved with gold, but in reality, they were paved with food markets, where "new arrivals could spend less money for much more food in greater variety." Certainly, pushcarts were not the only form of commerce supported by the immigrant community. But the immigrants were stratified, and many could not avail themselves of the bakeries, delicatessens and butchers that sprang up in their communities. For those who could, the choices abound. According to Moses Rischin in the *Promised City: New York Jews*, an 1899 survey revealed that "in the Jewish immigrant enclave there were 631 food mongers that catered to the needs of the inhabitants of the area. Most numerous were the 140 groceries, 131 butchers, 36 bakeries, 9 bread stands, 14 butter and egg stores, 24 candy stores, 7 coffee shops, 10 delicatessens, 9 fish stores, 7 fruit stands, 2 meat markets, 10 sausage stores, 13 wine shops, 13 grape wine shops and 10 confectioners."

However, it was the pushcart vendor who truly shaped the foodways of the city. Pushcart peddling was a common occupation back in the old country,

Bustling Hester Street, circa 1903. *National Archives and Records Administration.*

especially after laws in eastern Europe, like the May Laws of 1880/1881 in Russia, prohibited Jews from owning or renting land. Pushcarts, a non-stationary form of trade, allowed Jews to conduct business without breaking the law. Once in America, immigrants took up their practiced trades, and with a little luck and a lot of hard work, the pushcart vendor of 1880 could become the appetizing store owner of 1900. One could obtain a pushcart with just a small investment. Proceeds earned could then be rolled into a brick-and-mortar business. Deborah Dash Moore in *Jewish New York* reported that it cost only ten cents per day to rent the cart, and the inventory could be bought on credit. The typical pushcart was eight feet long and four feet wide. Stationary carts had two wheels and a pole that would provide stability. The first pushcarts were set up on Hester Street in 1866, creating an expansive open-air market. The *New York Tribune* wrote in 1898:

> *The neighborhood of Hester, Norfolk and Essex Streets presents a quaint scene. The streets are black with purchasers, and bright with the glare of hundreds of torches from pushcarts....The voices of the peddlers crying their wares...the mingling of the Yiddish of the elders with the English of the young people.*

Jacob Riis in his groundbreaking and frank depiction of *How the Other Half Lives*, described the sometimes chaotic pushcart scene: "The crowds that jostle each other at the wagons and about the sidewalk shops, where a gutter plank does the duty for a counter! Pushing, struggling, babbling, and shouting in foreign tongues; a veritable Babel of confusion." By 1900, the city had close to 2,500 pushcarts, with Jewish vendors comprising the largest numbers. They lined the streets, providing convenience for these new immigrants who had neither access, lingual skills nor funds for other options. Well-to-do shoppers would also shop, either in need of their wares or as a weekend outing from other parts of the city. While the local community viewed pushcarts as their lifeline, not everyone was a fan. Some viewed the pushcarts as unsanitary, despite governmental inspections that proved otherwise. Many local shopkeepers, who might have been pushcart vendors themselves at one time, would complain that they blocked their entrances and clogged the streets. Food historian Andrew F. Smith reported that laws were developed stating that the vendor had to relocate every thirty minutes. Imagine if your favorite food truck of today had to do the same? The law proved unenforceable, so open-air markets were mandated, sometimes stretching up to fourteen blocks. Soon the city began issuing licenses to try to restrict the pushcarts, but they had an uphill battle. By 1906, Mayor George McClellan had formed a pushcart commission to regulate the nearly four thousand legal vendors. Corruption was commonplace, as vendors bribed police officers to look the other way, while they would corral their carts like pioneers circling the wagons.

Many viewed the pushcart pushback as part of a larger anti-immigrant sentiment. There were those who feared these newcomers, who differed from previous immigrants, as they did not come from northern and western European English-speaking countries. The southern and eastern Europeans were viewed as true outsiders, and laws to restrict their influx in great numbers were enacted in 1921 and 1924. This coincided with the crackdown on the pushcart trade. Historians view the two as an effort to restrict the eastern and southern European immigrants, curb their influence and even dissuade more from emigrating. However, pushcart vendors persevered and proved invaluable during the Depression, providing cheap food such as potatoes and apples to those who were struggling financially.

All that changed in 1939, when New York was chosen as the site for the World's Fair. Mayor Fiorello La Guardia, who was always opposed to pushcart vending, now had the impetus to truly restrict it. He used federal funding to create indoor markets, the most well-known being the Essex Street Market, still operational today. Gone were the carts that dotted the streets as new, shiny, more Americanized indoor versions took their place. Street peddling was essentially outlawed, but not for long. In 1941, merchants on Orchard Street found that without the pushcarts, their business declined.

A Depression-era pushcart vendor selling baked potatoes on the street. *NYPL, Miriam and Ira D. Wallach Division of Art, Prints and Photographs.*

Absent were the local shoppers and tourists who would come to the Lower East Side for bargains and to see the famed pushcart vendors. So once again they began to appear, and they remain a presence in the city today. The pushcart vendors of the 1800s to 1900s laid the groundwork for the proliferation of delicatessens, appetizing stores and major food brands associated with the city. Their influences set the benchmark for the foods that would become integral to New York as many of the trends that followed in the tire tracks and footprints of those first pushcarts and peddlers gained iconic status.

~~~

Pushcart Puppies

(Reprinted with permission by The Kosher Carnivore, *June Hersh, St. Martin's Press, 2011.)*

The pushcarts of New York were and are still famous for their hot dogs, something that was peddled more than one hundred years ago and continue to be iconic to the streets of New York. This recipe takes the hot dog and encases it in another pushcart favorite: the pretzel. It's great for game day or as the perfect pickup food. Horns honking and traffic lights optional.

Makes 10.

For the Dough:

1 cup lukewarm water (about 110 to 115°F)
1 tablespoon brown sugar
1 tablespoon active dry yeast
1 teaspoon kosher salt
3 cups all-purpose flour
2 tablespoons margarine (butter if you do not need it pareve), melted

For the Hot Dog:

8 cups water
½ cup baking soda
10 fat knockwurst or dinner-size hot dogs, patted dry

For the Egg Wash:

1 egg beaten with 1 teaspoon water
Coarse salt

Combine the water, sugar and yeast in the bowl of a standing mixer. Gently stir and let the yeast bubble for 10 minutes. After that time, add the salt, flour and melted margarine or butter. Place the bowl on the mixer, fitted with the dough hook, and combine on low speed for 30 seconds; increase to medium speed until all ingredients are well combined and the dough completely pulls away from the side of the bowl, about 3 minutes.

Turn the dough out onto a clean surface and knead for 1 minute longer. If the dough is sticky, add a touch more flour. Place the dough in a large bowl that has been lightly greased with vegetable oil. Cover with plastic wrap and let the dough rise in a warm spot for about one hour, until roughly double in size.

While the dough rises, fill a large pot with the water and baking soda and bring to a boil. Line a baking sheet with parchment paper and preheat the oven to 450 degrees. After an hour, turn the dough out onto a lightly floured work surface. Divide the dough into ten equal pieces. Take a piece of dough and roll or stretch it to a 4-to-5-inch circle. Place the hot dog in the center of the circle and roll the dog so it is completely wrapped in the dough (the ends can peek out). Repeat with the remaining hot dogs and dough.

Drop one hot dog at a time into the boiling water and boil for 40–50 seconds. Remove with a slotted spoon, shake off the water and place on the lined baking sheet, seam side down. Repeat with all hot dogs. Brush each with egg wash and sprinkle with kosher salt or everything bagel seasoning.

Bake for 12 minutes or until the dough is a golden brown. Serve whole as a pickup food or slice on the diagonal for smaller bites. Dunk liberally in spicy brown mustard.

THE HOLE STORY

BAGELS

Did you hear the one about the employee who had to take a drug test? He was told they found opiates in his sample. He explained it must have been from the poppy seeds on his bagel. When they asked about the other drugs that were detected he quickly replied, "It was an everything bagel!"

O n a bitterly cold February day, when only the boldest tourist or most foolish New Yorker would be out and about, I positioned myself at the corner of 81st and Central Park West. There the subway line unites New Yorkers and tourists alike at a major crossroads of the Upper West Side. I posed a simple question to anyone I could engage: "What do you consider to be the quintessential New York food?" The responses contained the usual suspects: a pastrami sandwich, a slice of pizza or an indulgent sliver of creamy cheesecake. But by far the answer I heard most often was the bagel. This time-honored bread came to our shores with the wave of Jewish immigrants settling in New York's Lower East Side. It has worked its way into our collective soul as we savor nostalgia in every toothsome bite. Because of its distinct association with New York, instead of the moniker being the Big Apple, it should really be the Everything Bagel.

FLOUR POWER

When the bagel arrived on our shores, it came with a storied pedigree and had already appeared in many cultures throughout Europe and Asia. Italy's

The bagel's culinary cousin, fresh-baked taralli. *Romario99, Pixabay.*

version, which is still a popular snack, is called taralli, and it originated in the Puglia region of southern Italy. It was peasant food, created from scraps of leftover dough, shaped into a small ring. After the dough rose, they would briefly be tossed in hot water and then baked. It was especially crispy and had a crunchy quality. It is possible that this version was the first example of the modern bagel, as it appeared in writings dating back to the eighth century. Some posit that merchants traveling through the region brought the taralli back home with them or that the Jews of Puglia carried the recipe with them when they immigrated to eastern Europe.

In her comprehensive book *The Bagel: The Surprising History of a Modest Bread*, Maria Balinska noted that it was in the thirteenth century that Jewish tradesmen began to arrive in Krakow, Poland, from Germany and brought with them the German pretzel. The Yiddish word for this bread was *beigen*, which aptly means "to bend." Soon after came the *obwarzanek* (if you think an overstuffed sesame bagel is a mouthful, try saying that three times fast). This Krakow version came closest to the bagel as we know it today. The bread was boiled first and then baked and was said to be a favorite of the Polish queen Jadwiga when she reigned in the late fourteenth century. There's a very plausible theory as to why the Jewish bakers decided to boil the *obwarzanek*. A restrictive set of laws enacted by the church in Medieval Europe decreed that Jews could not bake, touch or buy bread. It is widely considered that clever Jewish bakers found a loophole by boiling the bread first, in the same way taralli were boiled before baking.

The first written documentation of the bagel came in 1610, when the Jewish Council of Krakow issued a set of regulations guiding the Jewish residents. Leo Rosten, in his *Joys of Yiddish*, noted that these "Sumptuary

A triumphant King Jan III Sobieski. Could those be bagels in his satchel? *Library of Congress, Prints and Photographs Division.*

Laws" covered many aspects of Jewish life, and the bagel got a special shout-out. His interpretation concluded that while bagels could be handed out to women in childbirth, they should otherwise be considered an indulgent luxury reserved for special celebrations such as a bris. Could that be the reason bagels are served at this lifecycle event even today?

Despite all these scholarly references to the bagel's heritage, how is it that a debunked anecdotal legend involving a Polish king and an Austrian baker is still the one many point to when talking about the birth of the bagel? The story says that a local baker in seventeenth-century Austria created the first true bagel as a gift to honor Jan Sobieski III, the king of Poland. The Viennese baker created a yeasty dough and shaped it to resemble a horse's stirrup, as the king was a passionate equestrian. This boiled and then baked bread looked much like our bagel of today. The Austrian word for stirrup is *beugel*, so you can see with manipulating just a few letters you arrive at our current spelling, albeit inspired from a fabled story.

Making Dough and a Living Too

Once the bagel landed in New York, it had all the makings of a *Dateline* story. There were union fights, poverty-stricken heroes, Socialist agitators and a widespread famine. As immigrants settled on the LES, they clung to the trades they knew best and were in search of comforting foods to buy and sell. While challah and matzo were religious breads, the bagel was a commonplace and secular one that this Ashkenazi community embraced. Without an angel investor or Kickstarter campaign, it's not easy to launch a startup. But that is just what these immigrants did. As Balinska noted, with a few hundred dollars, an oven and a basement, they could begin producing bagels to meet the rising demand for this familiar, inexpensive bread. While men provided the baking labor, working sometimes sixteen hours a day, it was young boys and older women who provided distribution. Harkening back to their days in eastern Europe, the peddlers would load the bagels onto long wooden dowels and sell them on the street. It wasn't uncommon to see ropes of up to five dozen bagels dangling like necklaces from the doors of a grocery, as the peddlers met the store's daily quota. Demand required constant replenishing, as a fresh bagel only stays that way for several hours.

Being a baker proved to be a difficult and challenging career path. In his book *The Jewish Unions in America*, Bernard Weinstein, who immigrated to New York in 1882, gave us a firsthand view of the Jewish baker's plight. He described deplorable living and working conditions. Most of the shops were located under Hester and Rivington Streets, with oppressive conditions. Low ceilings and little ventilation gave rise to the dough as well as temperatures of 120 degrees. Reports of half-clothed bakers, kneading the tough dough with their feet, created an image of laborers who toiled to feed the masses. The cramped space could barely hold the laborers needed to make the bagels, which consisted of a four-man crew. In his piece for

A 1910 painting depicting a bazaar in Russia with bagels strung on cords, dangling from the kiosk. *Wikimedia Commons.*

the *Harvard Review* (2005), Matthew Goodman described the process for making a bagel in the early 1900s:

> *The foreman of the crew was the ovenman, whose job it was to coax properly baked bagels from the demanding, difficult-to-regulate coal- or wood-fired ovens then two men worked as benchmen, or "rollers," cutting, rolling, and forming the dough into rings. The raw bagels were picked up by the kettleman, who dropped them into a huge vat of boiling water and then carried them to the ovenman for the baking.*

So dire were their conditions that a Yiddish expression emerged: *Lig in der un bak beygl.* Even with my cursory understanding of Yiddish (a necessary skill my sister and I learned at our family dinner table), I knew that this was a curse, not a blessing. It translates to "Lay in the ground and bake bagels." Essentially: go to hell!

Rather than quietly enduring these untenable conditions, the bakers would meet in local beer halls to vent their views, with copies of *The Forward*, the widely read Socialist-leaning Yiddish newspaper, firmly in hand. Local 31, the Jewish Baker's Union, was an outgrowth, and over the years the workers enacted several strikes pressing for labor reform. By 1907, there was a dedicated *Beigel* Bakers Union, designed solely to protect their rights. After one successful strike led by the union to improve conditions, Balinska described nearly five thousand people parading through the streets hoisting a fifteen-foot-long bread in defiant triumph.

Above: Bain News Service published this photo of triumphant workers carrying a loaf of bread in what it termed a "Socialist Parade." *Library of Congress, Prints and Photographs Division.*

Opposite: A 1951 ad for *Bagels and Yox. NYPL, Digital Collection.*

The unions continued to wield their power, and in the 1930s, three hundred bakers joined together to form Local 338, the longest-running bagel union. Membership did have its privileges, and it was very restrictive. Much like a cherished timepiece, entry was handed down from one generation to the next; a three- to six-month apprenticeship was mandated, and the ability to roll between 700 and 830 bagels per hour was required. These artisans protected their craft, and Local 338 had a monopoly on contracts with most of the local bagel shops. This union set the benchmark for other labor unions not only in New York but also throughout the country.

In the 1950s, without a single TikTok video, bagels were beginning to catch on to a wider demographic. Assuming that the bread was unfamiliar to its readers, the *New York Times* offered a pronunciation guide for the word ("baygle") and called it "a form of Jewish baked goods sometimes described as a doughnut with rigor mortis." It was becoming a common weekend breakfast ritual in New York City, where upward of 1 million bagels were

sold to be enjoyed for Saturday and Sunday morning brunch. It was a real blow to New Yorkers when, in 1951, Local 338 went on strike and the city experienced its first bagel famine. The strike had a ripple effect throughout New York, even affecting a Broadway show. The musical revue *Bagels and Yox* distributed bagels and cream cheese to its audience during intermission.

Because of the strike, the unthinkable occurred: it resorted to handing out donuts to disappointed theater goers.

The *Daily News* even reported attempts for New York restaurants to secure bootlegged bagels from New Jersey to fill the void. The smoked fish business also suffered, as lox sales plummeted to half of its normal amount. Natasha Frost in her article "The Forgotten History of New York's Bagel Famines" noted that the strike was settled by the State Board of Mediation's Murray Nathan, who had settled the lox strike of 1947. Sunday mornings were saved. By the 1960s, bagels were becoming not just a Jewish food, but rather a food associated with all New Yorkers. The *Times* declared that New York City was "the bagel center of the free world and will doubtless be kept that way by the hundreds of thousands of residents who find that a bagel makes breakfast almost worth getting up for." According to Frost, New York's bagel bakers were churning out 250,000 bagels per day. The union had a tight hold on the industry and wielded its full weight in 1962 when it went on strike for twenty-nine days and caused the bagel famine felt around the city. Six other unions joined in the strike, with thousands of bakers refusing to work. Bagel production was down by 85 percent, and even the *Daily News* quipped, "Now that King Saud has left, maybe President Kennedy can do something about the bagel strike." Their demands were finally met, and it seemed that the bagel workers were untouchable.

That was until Harry Lender changed the bagel making world forever. When Lender immigrated to the States from Lublin, Poland, in 1927, he had the unmitigated gall to work in a bagel bakery *outside* New York, in Passaic, New Jersey. Eventually, he established his own bakery in New Haven, Connecticut, ironically calling it the New York Bagel Bakery. Lender revolutionized the production of bagels first by freezing them and then pre-slicing them, eventually shifting away from baking them in open flat ovens. Lender was a great marketer of his product and was known to address the question of whether the bagel was a Jewish bread with this explanation: "A bagel has a versatility. When most people call it a Jewish product, it hurts us….If you must be ethnic, you can call it a Jewish English muffin with personality." Lender can definitely be credited with bagelising the country. To that end, the real bagel breakthrough (or demise) came when Lender leased a bagel making machine from inventor Daniel Thompson. At his plant in Illinois, according to Balinska, Lender could churn out 1 million bagels per day. Bagels were now mass-produced and widely distributed, and the art of hand rolling remained for the purists.

B-Bomb Hits N. Y. — a Bagel Strike

By HARRY SCHLEGEL

A wave of consternation akin to panic spread among the gourmands and gourmets of New York yesterday. A strike-inspired bagel famine hit the metropolitan area, and tens of thousands of bagel lovers, as emotional a group of fanatics as you could find, were threatening the bagel-eater's equivalent of mass hara-kiri if the strike isn't settled by the weekend.

Newcomers in the delicatessen industry, which sells most of the bagels, tried to palm off substitutes, but it was a waste of time. Your true bageler, like a one-man dog, is a creature of iron will and deep loyalty, bolstered by a firm conviction that only a bagel, preferably garnished with cream cheese and lox, is a fit breakfast for a civilized human. And on Sunday it's double in spades.

While the Supply Lasted.

The strike began at 12:01 A.M. last Saturday, but by that time enough bagels had been delivered to bagel-bins in the lower East Side, Brooklyn, Washington Heights and the Bronx to take care of a sizable fraction of the normal demand.

Those who missed out on their bagels last Sunday apparently thought the shortage was due to a sudden demand caused by a marked increase of bagel fanciers. The thought of a strike never hit them.

It was only yesterday that the carefully guarded secret leaked out. Philip Levine, attorney for the Bagel Bakers Association of New York, a revered group of 27 of the city's 29 bagel maestros, admitted that 32 of the 34 bakeries qualified to turn out the succulent tooth-breakers was closed down. Some 40 bagel-truck drivers, mem-

bers of Local 802 of the AFL teamsters union, were on strike, he said, with little likelihood of a quick settlement.

Just the Ersatz Stuff.

A confirmed bagel-eater never worries about his supply until he knows he cannot buy any, and Levine's reluctant admission had the gustatory impact of a hydrogen bomb. Customers rushed to delicatessens, to find that only egg bagels, made of egg-enriched flour, or Bialystok bagels, onion-encrusted rolls with slight dents in them, were on sale. The true water bagel, shaped roughly like a doughnut and with the general consistency of high-grade cement, was nowhere to be seen.

By mid-afternoon the sale of

lox, the orange-reddish smoked salmon which is to bagels what ham is to eggs, and cream cheese had dropped an estimated 50%, and delegations of bagelers were planning a protest parade to City Hall.

The drivers, who get a guaranteed minimum wage of $108 for a six-day week, want a pay rise of $12, plus a third week's vacation, and overtime pay after eight hours for their Friday night-Saturday shift, when they often work up to 15 or more hours at a stretch, they complain. Their strike has idled 250 bakers, who are members of Local 338 of the AFL Bakery and Confectionery Workers Union.

A Vicious Bagel Circle.

Levine points out that higher wage costs will mean higher prices for bagels, which in turn may result in less demand, shrinking job opportunities and a gradual decline in the industry. Bagel plants, he said, have already absorbed many added costs, without jumping the price of the products, and cannot take another extra tax without passing it on to the ultimate chewer.

This argument met a cool reception at the union. Its business agent is a man with the unbagel-like name of Robert J. (Paddy) Sullivan.

FIG. 2

U.S. Patent

Mar. 28, 1995

Sheet 2 of 3

5,400,702

Above: A *Daily News* article likens the bagel strike to a panic-driven famine. *Newspapers.com.*

Left: John Lugo headed R&D for Lender's Bagels and was the father of frozen bagels and inventor of this bagel turning machine. *Wikimedia Commons.*

H^2 OH!

What makes a New York bagel? There are bagel shops across the country and the world, and many sell "New York–style bagels." I liken that to being a "little bit pregnant." Either you're a New York bagel or you're not. So, what is the main qualification for being a true New York bagel? Many would argue that it's in the water. It seems even the Smithsonian gives credence to that theory. In its article "How Chemistry Gives New York City Bagels an Edge," Helen Thompson reported on the work of chemist Noel Waghorn. Waghorn acknowledged that city water doesn't come from the city, but it is proprietary to New York, as it flows from Upstate in the Catskill Mountains through specific terrain. The Catskill aqueduct is part of the New York City water supply, bringing mountain water to Yonkers, where it is then distributed throughout the city. Construction began in 1907 and was totally finished in 1924. It was reported to cost $177 million at the time, which today would be in excess of $5 billion. Waghorn explained what makes this billion-dollar water so valuable:

> [It is] *particularly soft and has low levels of calcium and magnesium. Ratios of these minerals in water affect the gluten in the bagel dough. New York's water is a bit like the Goldilocks of bagel water chemistry; just the right softness, creating just the right degree of tenderness and chewiness.*

The water is so integral to creating the perfect bagel that the New York City Department of Environmental Protection published the following on its website:

> *When Steve Ross of the Coney Island Bialy and Bagel Bakery was invited to participate in the Smithsonian Institute's 2001 Folklife Festival, he brought 36 gallons of New York City drinking water with him to ensure that the bialys and bagels would be the perfect examples of these New York specialties. When the New York City Department of Environmental Protection (DEP) heard that Mr. Ross was running low because he had "loaned" some to the pickle and herring purveyors, Russ & Daughters, DEP air lifted another 20 gallons to the festival.*

To discover all the elements that make a perfect bagel, I consulted bagel expert Mike Varley. How do you become a bagel expert, you might wonder? Mike earned it by walking five marathons a week in a thirteen-month period

This 1911 photo appeared in *Cassier's Magazine* showing the construction of the Catskill Aqueduct. *Wikimedia Commons.*

(that's seven thousand miles) through all five boroughs of New York. To offset the calories he burned, he stopped at 202 bagel shops during his journey and sampled the same combo at each: an everything bagel with scallion cream cheese. He then used a ranking and scored the best bagels in each borough (for his results, visit www.everythingiseverything.nyc). Mike imparted this advice: "A good bagel is a variety from bite to bite, one might be doughy, then toasty like a nice baguette crunch. Each bite should tell a different story." When I visited an artisan bagel maker, I tasted the difference in an authentically prepared bagel that is hand rolled, kettle boiled and hearth baked. The bagel shop smelled yeasty, the bagel's color was golden and the bite was toothsome. It's this multisensory moment that defines the quintessential New York bagel experience. The first ingredient for an artisanal bagel maker is patience. They need to let the dough rest, sometimes up to a day, to allow the gluten to relax and the yeast to fulfill its fermenting destiny. Then they should hand roll, which creates bagels with personality; a center hole that allows for even baking; a smaller, tighter shape; and a crumb that benefits from the human touch. If every bagel in the bin looks the same, they weren't hand rolled. Beware the perfect bagel.

Next, kettle boiling is a must, often with a touch of malt or baking soda, which does several things. It creates that lacquer-like exterior, a surface that allows toppings to cling and a crunch that is audible. The last step is to hearth bake, usually on a wooden plank covered in layers of burlap. Bagel bakers say that the best time to eat a bagel is fifteen minutes before you order it! After that, the bagel would make a good doorstop, but not a delicious nosh. So, look for a bagel shop that replenishes regularly. If they strongly

Well-rested dough is portioned and ready to roll. *Photo by author.*

Look for full bins of imperfect bagels; like snowflakes, no two should be alike. *Photo by author.*

suggest you toast your bagel, it means they might not be fresh. Writing in the *New York Times*, food guru Ed Levine suggested that "a bagel should weigh four ounces or less and should make a slight cracking sound when you bite into it instead of a whoosh." He went on to say, "A bagel should be eaten warm and, ideally, should be no more than four or five hours old when consumed. Bagels do not need six ounces of cream cheese…only a schmear…and a buttered bagel should almost always be toasted." In a nod to exotic flavor combinations, Levine obviously favors a purist approach: "If God had wanted sun-dried tomatoes put into bagels, he would have put more bagel bakers in Italy."

The Schmear

Let's play a game of geographic word association. If someone says "mozzarella," you'd answer Italy. Jarlsberg conjures visions of the Swiss Alps. Say "cream cheese" and the answer, of course, is the city of Philadelphia,

Just ordinary breakfast toast becomes an *extra*-ordinary treat when you set out Philadelphia Brand Cream Cheese to spread on it along with the jelly or jam!

There's a delicate richness, an exquisitely *fresh* flavor that goes great at breakfast. And Philadelphia Brand Cream Cheese is a wholesome treat, too; it gives the family food energy, vitamin A plus other important milk and cream nutrients.

Taste cool, creamy Philadelphia Brand on hot breads, waffles and pancakes, too. Delicious! Just be sure it's *genuine* Philadelphia Brand you buy—the brand made only by Kraft and *guaranteed fresh*. Whenever you shop for cream cheese always *see* the words "Philadelphia Brand" *printed* on every package.

Copr. 1948 by Kraft Foods Company

This Kraft cream cheese ad appeared in the *Ladies' Home Journal* in 1948. *Wikimedia Commons.*

right? Not so fast. Cream cheese, the schmearable creamy cow's milk cheese that we slather on bagels, was created in New York by one William Lawrence in 1872. According to Jewish food historian and author Gil Marks, Lawrence accidentally created the ubiquitous topper by adding too much heavy cream when trying to replicate Neufchâtel, a soft French cheese. His dairy was purchased in 1880, and they branded the product Philadelphia Cream Cheese. Marks posits that it could have been paying homage to an Upstate town called Philadelphia, New York, or perhaps to elevate the product, they gave it the name of a city associated with fine dining. To keep up with demand, in 1907, the Breakstone brothers, who emigrated from Lithuania to New York, began manufacturing their version from a small factory in Brooklyn. Cream cheese became a go-to ingredient for baking rugelach and cheesecake, but it was its role as part of the triumvirate—bagels, lox and cream cheese—that made the three components inseparable. The origins of that trio are truly unknown, but Jewish food authority Joan Nathan suggested that it came from a Philadelphia Cream Cheese ad campaign. Kraft Foods, which owned the brand and was a sponsor of a radio show, encouraged its entertainers, such as Al Jolson, to sing the praises of cream cheese and work it into some of their "Jewish" jokes.

The Earth Might Be Round, but a Bialy Is Flat

I would be remiss if I didn't give a nod to the bialy, the underappreciated, less famous sibling of the bagel. Their DNA is similar, combining high-gluten flour, water and yeast, but their history, shape, preparation and texture are complete departures. Much like the bagel, bialys arrived in America with Polish Jewish immigrants. They had been a staple of their Ashkenazi heritage and came by their name naturally, as they were born in Bialystok. Its full name is *bialystocker kuchen*, Yiddish for "little bread from Bialystok." Unlike bagels, bialys have no hole in the center; rather, they have an indentation filled with tiny bits of caramelized onion, garlic or poppy seeds, which lends another layer of flavor to the simple dough. Bialys do not take a swim in a steamy bath before being baked, so they have less of a crust and more of a slightly dense outer layer contrasting with the pillowy soft center. The greatest difference between the bagel and the bialy is that the bialy needs better PR, as it has not reached the same fame outside of New York as the bagel. That makes it more iconically New York because if you want to enjoy the true taste of a freshly baked bialy, you'll most likely

Fresh-baked bialys at Kossar's Bakery. *Photo by author.*

have to pay a visit to the city. When you do, be sure to make Kossar's your bialy stop. The bakery was founded in 1936 on the LES by Russian immigrants Morris Kossar and Isadore Mirsky. The store concept was to sell just a single product, so they must have been confident that it would be very good. The store thrived and became the premier bakery of New York–style bialys. Like so many other tales from the LES involving unions and strikes, Kossar's was once embroiled in a labor union matter. The bakery left the Bialy Bakers Association, and in retaliation, a suspicious explosion destroyed a portion of the bakery. Luckily, no one was injured and Kossar's reopened. It remains the oldest operating bialy bakery in the country. My visit to Kossar's revealed bialys not just dotted with onion and garlic but also versions with sun-dried tomato filling, olives or sesame seeds. One of the bakers told me that they debuted a whole wheat version, but with little success, as customers favor the original. She feels that they bake and sell at least one thousand bialys per day. Today, the shop is owned by Marom Unger, who says that the bakery's founder wanted "to feed people a little bit of home." And for more than eighty years, that's what Kossar's has been doing. *New York Times* food critic Mimi Sheraton wrote of their bialys, "I knew Kossar's to be the source of the very best bialys in the city and as it turned out, the entire country."

A BAKER'S DOZEN OF FUN FACTS ABOUT HOLE FOODS

Wondering what the most popular flavor of bagel is? According to a 2022 Grubhub survey in New York, the answer is the everything bagel, adorned with black and white sesame seeds, poppy seeds, dried onion, dried garlic and sea salt. Coming in not too far behind are the blueberry, cinnamon raisin and jalapeño. Nationwide, you might be surprised that blueberry tops the list.

According to the website Eat This, Not That, the everything bagel just might owe its discovery to a fifteen-year-old bagel worker in Howard Beach, New York, who claims that he created the bagel after seeing all the leftover seeds when cleaning out the oven. He combined them all, and voilà!

What was the largest bagel ever made? Try taking a bite out of a whopping 868-pound bagel made by Brueggers Bagels, which was presented at a state fair in Geddes, New York, in August 2004. That most certainly was a handmade bagel, but the machinery to produce bagels has come a long way. Thompson's original machine could turn out four hundred per hour, but the new models can create up to five thousand per hour.

H&H bagels, one of the most well-known bagel shops in the city, got its name not because the family members were Hymie and Harold. It was named by the two owners, Helmer Toro and his brother-in-law, Hector Hernandez, in 1972, when these entrepreneurial Puerto Rican–born bakers established their first bagel shop.

If you ate a bagel in 2022, you're not alone. According to Statista, 202.7 million Americans admit to scarfing down a bagel that year, while 127.33 million shied away from the carbs. The number of bagel lovers has steadily increased from 2011, with a continued increase projected through 2024.

If you're counting calories, then avoid the bagels the size of a life preserver. Those can have as many as 600 to 1,000 calories, and that's before a schmear of cream cheese. According to the USDA, a medium plain bagel (about 3.5 to 4 inches in diameter) contains about 277 calories, about three times as many as a single slice of bread. A good tip is to order a kid's size mini bagel to get your fix—that usually has under 100 calories.

Even Daniel Thompson's automated bagel maker could not keep up with today's bagel demands. *Wikimedia Commons.*

A nod to nostalgia is depicted in this illustration showing the dowels that were used to stack and tote fresh-baked bagels. *Jean-Pierre Thimot, Shutterstock.*

Would you ever imagine that William Shatner and the bagel had anything in common, except both having Jewish lineage? Add to that: they've both been to space! Astronaut Gregory Chamitoff brought eighteen sesame bagels (albeit from a Montreal bakery) with him on a 2008 space journey.

You don't have to be a rocket scientist to understand why a bagel has a hole in the center. It creates a largest surface area for more crust formation, while allowing the heat to circulate better and cook the bagel faster. Also, it's handy for the peddlers who toted bagel-laden dowels.

Would it surprise you to know that Dunkin' Donuts sells the most bagels of any national food chain? I suppose sometimes you just want a bagel with your coffee instead of a French cruller.

Speaking of coffee, Einstein Bagels now makes a buzzed bagel. Its espresso bagel contains 32mg of caffeine, about one-third the amount in a cup of coffee. Now when you're in a rush, you can clear your morning fog and hunger in one bite.

If you've been coaxed into buying a rainbow bagel by your kids, you're not alone. The invention of Brooklyn baker Scot Rossillo came more than two decades ago and continues to be a hit. As for taste, this highly Instagrammable bagel that looks like Play-Doh tastes just like a regular bagel, as the food coloring adds no actual flavor.

We celebrate the bagel every year on January 15, as this humble bread that arrived on our shores more than one hundred years ago has earned its own day.

~~~

Bagel Chips with Everything Bagel Scallion Dip

You can toast day-old bagels and enjoy them with butter, but two-day-old bagels are only good as hockey pucks. Or you could turn them into crispy golden bagel chips. Just beware: they are sneakily addictive. To complete the duo, make a simple dip to dunk your freshly baked chips. You can use full-fat or low-fat ingredients—it's your waistline and decision. This combo takes the bagel and a schmear to the next level.

Makes about 2 dozen bagel chips.

For the Bagel Chips:

Stale bagel(s) (for best results, one to five days old)
Olive oil
Sea salt

For the Dip:

1 cup (8 ounces) cream cheese, room temperature
1 cup (8 ounces) sour cream or plain yogurt
1 tablespoon chopped scallion (about 2 small scallions, white and light green parts only)
2–3 tablespoons everything bagel seasoning (available at Trader Joe's, most markets and online), or follow the simple recipe below.

Homemade bagel chips with everything seasoning and dip for dunking. *Photo by author.*

How to cut your bagel for the perfect bite-sized chips. *Photo by author.*

Preheat the oven to 350°F and set aside a rimmed baking sheet. If you're making a big batch, you'll need several sheets.

Cut the bagels in half down the middle, not through the equator, as you would normally slice them, and then cut each in half again. Starting at the end, using a serrated knife, slice the bagel into thin slices about ⅛-inch thick.

Place the slices on the rimmed baking sheet and lightly drizzle olive oil on the bagels; then sprinkle with a touch of sea salt and toss to coat. Arrange in a single layer. If you are making the dip, you can leave the salt off the chips, as the dip is heavily seasoned. For a healthier chip, you can also omit the oil. For a cinnamon raisin or blueberry bagel, try pairing a warm spice like cinnamon.

Bake for about 15 minutes, or until the chips are a golden brown. Remove from the oven and let cool on a wire rack.

While the bagels bake, prepare the dip. Place the cream cheese, sour cream or yogurt in a small bowl and, using a handheld mixer, beat the two together on low speed until fully incorporated and creamy, about 15 seconds. Spoon in your everything seasoning to taste, adding as much or as little as you like (2–3 tablespoons is about right). Add scallions and chill until ready to use.

Homemade Everything Bagel Seasoning

You can easily create your own everything bagel seasoning, but it actually might save you money to buy it already prepared. Trader Joe's is everyone's favorite, but your local market will most likely have a version in the spice section. This recipe is a balance of all the ingredients, but feel free to add more of one and less of another based on your preferences.

Combine 1 tablespoon each black sesame seeds, white sesame seeds, dried minced garlic (do not substitute garlic salt or garlic powder, as it will fall to the bottom), dried minced onion flakes (same goes for this ingredient) and poppy seeds. Season with about 1 teaspoon sea or kosher salt or to taste. Store in a sealed container and use on everything!

SPAWNING A NEW FOOD OBSESSION

SMOKED, PICKLED AND BRINED FISH

*T*he Jewish immigrants of the early 1900s were in a pickle and had / a smoking habit. When the great influx from eastern Europe arrived in America, they brought the tradition of eating pickled and smoked fish with them. This included smoked salmon, herring, whitefish, sturgeon, sable, trout and mackerel. Smoked food has been around for centuries, since Greek and Roman times. Because smoking any food preserves it, as well as adds another layer of flavor, it's been a technique that most cultures have practiced, including New York's indigenous Lenapes. Like so many foods, it was one born out of necessity. When you combine long winters with a food that is easy to obtain, you find a way to make it last. By drying, smoking or pickling a food, you preserve it, extending its shelf life. The first reported smoking factory in Europe was in Poland during the seventh century, so we know that these new immigrants had the knowledge and expertise in this process. However, Claudia Roden in her compendium *The Book of Jewish Food* questioned whether the poor peasants in eastern Europe could have actually afforded salmon—more likely they cured, pickled and smoked lesser fish like herring or whitefish.

These offerings were now abundant and affordable in New York at the turn of the century, and Ashkenazi Jews couldn't get enough of them. Serious Eats writer Niki Achitoff-Gray gave a tongue-in-cheek explanation of the hierarchy of the smoked, brined and pickled fish that was popularized by these new New Yorkers:

> *In my family, you can measure the gravity of an event by the volume of smoked and pickled fish on the table. A casual brunch gets smoked salmon,*

While men trawled for herring, women known as the "Herring Girls" gutted and prepared them for export. *PL SSPL/East News*.

perhaps some pickled herring. For bar and bat mitzvahs, add whitefish salad and sable. Weddings and funerals? The big guns come out: whole smoked trout and mackerel, salty belly lox, flaky bluefish, even sturgeon and a prized bowl of caviar.

How Do You Prevent Your Bagel from Running Away? Put Lox on It!

Like any good relationship, each partner needs to bring something to the table. Bagels and lox are no different. In this relationship, one might wonder, who is the alpha? Do bagels need lox more, or does lox require a bagel? Unlike the bagel, lox might be the one voted most likely to need a friend. Bagels are routinely eaten on their own, and they don't need to fraternize with another food to be enjoyed. Lox, on the other hand, generally benefits from companionship. Before it began dating the bagel, lox was eaten on slabs of rye or pumpernickel coated in butter, and it was delicious. Food historians suggest that because Jewish brunch goers couldn't enjoy some more typical American specialties like ham and eggs, they created their own. The combo became so imbedded in what many felt was an assimilated Jewish experience that a common insult from one immigrant family to the next would be to call them "bagels and lox." Some feel it's cream cheese that holds this marriage together or that double dating with red onion and capers is healthy now and again. Lox settled down with the bagel in New York in the early 1900s,

"East and West Shaking Hands at Laying Last Rail." Photo taken in 1869 to commemorate the driving of the "golden stake" to complete the transcontinental railroad. *Yale University Library, Wikimedia Commons.*

and they have been together ever since. This certainly does not hinder lox's iconic status on its own. Lox is literally transformative, taking a humble piece of salmon and turning it into a star. The bagel was a bachelor until lox showed up. Here's how it got its start in America.

In 1869, the transcontinental railroad system was operational, facilitating a flow of goods from coast to coast that was impossible before its completion The Hudson Bay Company took advantage of the railway system and diversified its fur trading business. It began shipping, among other things, Pacific salmon, which it packed in salt and transported to the East Coast. The salt encasement "cured" the salmon, changing its taste and texture. With a plentiful supply of cured fish coming from the West, smokehouses sprang up in New York City. Smoked salmon became a ubiquitous commodity, newly accessible and affordable. What today could top fifty dollars per pound then cost thirty-six cents. Imagine the immigrant's delight that a food once reserved for the elite was now available to them.

Slicing paper-thin ribbons of smoked salmon requires a very sharp knife and a very skilled hand. *Russ & Daughters.*

A hub for smoked salmon developed in Brooklyn led by Acme Smoked Fish, established in 1906 by Russian immigrant Harry Brownstein. Brownstein would distribute smoked fish throughout the city in a horse-drawn wagon. The business went from distributing to production in 1954. Harry's great-granddaughter Emily Caslow, who is involved in the business, explained how the name Acme was chosen. She said it connotes "best in the business," but Harry also felt that it would be perfectly positioned in the Yellow Pages, ahead of one of his competitors, whose name began with a *B*. Today, Acme continues to supply most of the high-end appetizing stores with its smoked salmon and smoked fish products, and with wide supermarket distribution, it annually sells more than 20 million pounds of fish. To create its Guinness record-breaking bagel and lox, Acme used 30 pounds of Nova along with 40 pounds of cream cheese. The combo weighed in at 213.75 pounds and measured a whopping thirty-six by thirty-one inches. So how is it that one person swears their appetizing shop has the best smoked salmon, when the next prefers theirs if the fish comes from the same source? Emily's brother and co-CEO Adam Caslow feels that it is less about the fish and more about the slicing. To ensure you are getting the best bite of smoked salmon, make sure it is cut by hand in thin ribbons to release the oils and create the perfect buttery texture. Adam exuded pride when talking about the community connection saying, "It's crystal clear the type of comfort people are trying to find in a bagel and lox." If you haven't tried hand-sliced smoked salmon, New York is the place to do so. But beware, Adam warns, "Smoked salmon is a gateway drug to seafood."

Lox 101

When I was a child growing up in New Rochelle, a suburb north of the city, my Sunday mornings had a definite routine. My grandfather would make me a cup of coffee milk, which comprised a thimble full of coffee mixed with a cup of whole milk. The drink came in very handy to wash down the salty belly lox that we had for breakfast. Belly lox was the only lox I knew, popular among the new immigrants. In order for you to know exactly what you're ordering when you generically ask for lox, I offer this quick tutorial, which should help you become a lox maven in a New York minute.

The salty lox of my childhood, which is still available today, is cured with copious amounts of salt but not smoked, and it has a brackish taste. If you ask for lox next time you order, they might look at you quizzically and ask, "Are you sure?" Its bracing flavor is not for everyone, but as the forty-something Peter Shelsky of Shelsky's of Brooklyn told me, "It's my favorite, I'm an eighty-year-old Jew." The word *lox* derives from the Yiddish word *lachs*, which means salmon, so perhaps lox is the true, quintessential version. It's fatty and unctuous and should be tried. While definitely related, lox is to smoked salmon like basic table wine is to a 1946 Château Mouton-Rothschild.

Smoked salmon is exactly that. It is not just cured but cold smoked. Each smokehouse has its own method of preparing the fish for smoking, imparting different nuances of sweetness or saltiness depending on the dry rub or wet brine used. The result is a flavorful bite, less salty than lox with a silky mouthfeel. The term Nova ("novy" to those in the know) originally referred to the origin of the salmon used, coming from the waters off Nova Scotia, which is no longer always the case. Nova is most likely the salmon you are trying to order when you simply ask for lox. No matter where the fish spawned, it's referred to as Nova in most appetizing stores.

Wanting to learn more about the actual technique involved in smoking salmon led me to visit a smokehouse forty-five minutes outside the city. It was a fascinating and pungent experience. When you walk through the doors of Mount Kisco Smokehouse, you are immediately enveloped with a coat of smoke and the smells of burning wood shavings. The magic happens in the back room, where coarse salt was being applied to loins of salmon from the Faroe Islands, much like a massage therapist at the Four Seasons would stroke a pampered guest. After four days resting in the curing room, the salmon is salted once again for good measure and then cold-smoked for precisely one hundred minutes at a temperature of about seventy degrees Fahrenheit in a behemoth smoker whose name, fittingly, is The Titan.

Fishing for salmon has come a long way since this depiction sketched in the 1600s. *University of Toronto Wenceslas Hollar Digital Collection, Wikimedia Commons.*

The cured salmon is ready for a cold smoke. It goes in as belly lox and comes out as smoked salmon. *Photo by author.*

Above: As they say in New York, the slices of salmon should be so translucent you can read the *Sunday Times* through them. *Photo by author.*

Opposite: The dining room at the Concord Hotel was a cross between a college mess hall and Kellerman's from *Dirty Dancing*. *Library of Congress, John Margolies, Roadside America, photograph archive, Wikimedia Commons.*

Watching owner William slice the freshly smoked salmon is like watching a samurai with the precision of a surgeon. The long, thin knife glided through the salmon, certainly indicative of his forty-plus years of experience. The result was perfectly translucent slices of glistening pink deliciousness.

Salmon can also be cured with a salt and sugar mixture or hot smoked, both producing a very different texture compared to cold-smoked salmon. Gravlax is the result of curing with salt and sugar. The process takes several days, and the result is a more subtle slice with a somewhat elegant persona. It is not always available in a store, but it is often found on swanky restaurant menus; it's so easy to make at home. Hot smoking at 150 degrees creates kippered or baked salmon, with a drier texture and a distinctive smokey flavor. It's best sliced in thick strips and is perfect for flaking on top of a bagel or mashed into salmon salad. If you are really lucky, you will get to taste an often-neglected New York treat called pickled lox. To achieve its texture and taste, the lox is cut into chunks, brined, rinsed and then pickled with vinegar, spices and often onions. It gained true stardom at the Concord, one of New York State's iconic "Borscht Belt" hotels. According to a 1985 account by *New York Times* food writer Florence Fabricant:

> *Over the four days ending yesterday, which included the Rosh ha-Shanah holiday, about 7,200 portions of pickled lox were served at the Concord Resort Hotel in Kiamesha Lake, N.Y. Listed on the menu as "Fillet of*

marinated lox with Concord cream sauce and onion platter, sliced tomato," pickled lox is the most popular of the 120 or so dishes regularly served at the hotel.

At the time, the hotel estimated that since it began serving the dish in 1949, it had prepared 5 million portions. Fabricant cited comedic legends such as Alan King, Dom DeLuise and Joan Rivers as fans. Any New York appetizing store worth its long shiny counter will have all these varieties to choose from.

There Are Other Fish in the Sea

Herring might currently be the most underrated fish that New Yorkers devoured at the turn of the century. It was a staple in Poland, so much so that some there called herring "Jewish-style fish." It was said that the Poles ate a herring a day, with one writer commenting, "On Sunday one had a pickled herring, on Monday soused herring, on Wednesday baked herring, on Thursday herring fried in oatmeal and on Friday herring with sour cream." What they ate on Tuesday, Saturday and Sunday, I suppose, was a mystery. In case you are ever quizzed, here's a quick tutorial. *Schmaltz* herring is a very fatty fish that is caught just before it spawns, hence the name *schmaltz*, which in Yiddish means melted fat. It is cured with coarse salt for several days and then rinsed and sold as is or in a wine or cream sauce, with or without pickled onions or chopped into a salad often spiked with sweet apples. Matjes (meaning maiden) herring, the other most popular variety, are young and immature—that's not a critique but rather an observation. They are also called soused, which describes their long brining process, and the result is a milder herring. A third variety is most prized, called *Hollandse nieuwe* (Holland young herring). This Dutch delicacy is caught only from May to July and most likely was not available to the average immigrant in the early 1900s, but it is seasonally available now. Some feel that it is the premier herring experience, popping them directly into their mouths, tail in hand, head thrown back.

Herring became incredibly popular in New York, where they were sold from large barrels by pushcart vendors, one being Joel Russ, who went on to establish Russ & Daughters. His grandson Mark Russ Federman wrote in his book *Russ & Daughters: Reflections and Recipes from the House that Herring Built* that "pickled herring follows Jews of Eastern European background from the

Above: The prized *Hollandse nieuwe*. *Paul Einerhand, Unsplash.*

Left: The herring section at Russ & Daughters shows the breadth of herring available. *Russ & Daughters.*

cradle to the grave," as it's served from baby namings and brises to bar and bat mitzvahs through to weddings and funerals. The life of a herring vendor was not an easy one. Hordes of frugal shoppers would have the street vendor literally fish in a deep barrel for the one perfect herring they would buy. Niki Russ Federman, a fourth-generation owner of Russ & Daughters, said, "The streets of New York used to be filled with schmaltz herring mongers; this is what families ate." Another immigrant family, the Hellers, who arrived in New York from Czechoslovakia in 1898, were "savvy merchandisers on this culinary frontier," as herringmaven.blogspot.com noted. Their Yorkville deli

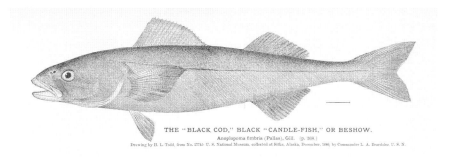

THE "BLACK COD," BLACK "CANDLE-FISH," OR BESHOW.
Anoplopoma fimbria (Pallas), Gill. (p. 268.)
Drawing by H. L. Todd, from No. 25745 U. S. National Museum, collected at Sitka, Alaska, December, 1880, by Commander L. A. Beardslee, U. S. N.

Top: This is an 1884 rendering of the sablefish, which is found mainly in Alaskan waters. It goes by many names; when cured, it is most known for its smooth taste and paprika-flecked coating. *University of Washington, Wikimedia Commons.*

Bottom: The regal sturgeon; feel free to weigh in on the scale debate. *W. Houghton, A.F. Lydon, Wikimedia Commons.*

prominently featured herring, and they decided to begin packaging it. From a small business, they established Vita Herring on Hudson Street and grew it to be a company that today is publicly traded. For the uninitiated, herring might seem like a slightly hairy, bristly fish not worth your time, but seek out an appetizing store that treats it like the delicacy it is and you'd be surprised how delicious a bite it can be.

Whitefish might just have more fans than herring, as it is the main ingredient in a salad made popular at the turn of the century. Ashkenazi Jews had eaten a variety of whitefish before immigrating to America, and it was a staple in the preparation of gefilte fish. When they arrived in America, they found that the Great Lakes offered up fish like those they had grown up eating—think cod-like—and when smoked, it quickly became a favorite among New Yorkers. It is often eaten as a whole smoked fish, which needs careful fileting, or bought as a chubb, a smaller deep-water variety. Its best friend is mayo, especially laced with dill, lemon, capers and celery to create whitefish salad. It is a staple at the appetizing counter and is perfect to top your bagel. This brings us to sable, a lesser-known smoked fish that is often enjoyed atop a bagel or sliced thin and savored for its mild buttery taste. Sable is a smoked version of black cod, noted by its paprika-tinged edges. Back in the day, it sold for seventy cents per pound and was loved by many. Federman quipped in 2001 to the *New York Times* about sable, "My grandfather would be rolling over in his grave….He had no clue the stuff he was selling was anything but Jewish peasant food. It always had a very déclassé aura."

Much more controversial than either sable or whitefish is the regal sturgeon. According to Professor Nancy Langston, you can date its origin to before the dinosaurs, having survived an extinction that wiped out 90 percent of living species. Any fish that tenacious deserves to be considered for iconic status. But sturgeon is not without controversy. Kosher laws dictate that only fish with scales easily removed can be eaten, and sturgeon kind of blurs that line. Religious writings and rabbis argued its classification, with some approving the sturgeon as kosher and others not. Despite a debate that involved a rabbi threatened with having his beard cut off as a penalty for heresy, many embrace this coveted fish for its slightly smokey, pinkish white flesh and mild, sweet taste. Like lox, sturgeon should be masterfully hand sliced, either in thin pieces that are translucent and can be folded onto a bagel or thick pieces that you need a knife and fork to cut. Mark Russ Federman recalled that while lox sold for thirty-five cents per pound in the early 1900s, sturgeon could garner up to a whopping four dollars per pound.

A re-creation of the Oscar-shaped smoked salmon edible statues topped with dollops of black caviar that fed A-listers at the 2022 Oscars. *Photo by author.*

As long as we're talking about the forbidden sturgeon, let's show a little love for its tiny pearl-shaped roe known as caviar, which Federman said "tastes as if the sea kissed your tongue." Not everyone finds the flavor or cost palatable, as an ounce of Osetra can set you back a whopping $100. While this delicacy was out of reach for most, the colorful tins would sit alongside all the aforementioned smoked delicacies in most appetizing stores. In a nod to the popularity of caviar among Jewish gourmands, now even the most observant can enjoy the pop of these salty fish eggs. Black Diamond, a Brooklyn-based caviar company, is marketing a "caviar-like" product harvested from the bowfin, a kosher fish. Finally, caviar for the masses—and kosher no less!

Homemade Gravlax

Here's how to transform a simple piece of Atlantic salmon into a delicacy.

Makes 2 pounds of gravlax.
Hands-on prep: 15 minutes
Total time: 2 to 3 days

2 (1-pound) pieces of Atlantic salmon, belly portion preferable
2 tablespoons chilled vodka
¼ cup kosher salt
¼ cup granulated sugar
Freshly cracked black pepper
1 bunch fresh dill weed
1 bunch fresh basil

Have your fishmonger cut two pieces of salmon that match up so that you can lay one on top of the other and they fit perfectly together. Cover a portion of your counter with enough plastic wrap to lay the salmon pieces down and then wrap them up. Place the salmon side by side, skin side down on the wrap. Drizzle each piece with 1 tablespoon of chilled vodka. Sprinkle both pieces with the salt and sugar mixture. Season with freshly cracked black pepper.

Lay enough dill and basil to cover the entire surface of both pieces. Using the plastic wrap as an aid, lay one piece of salmon over the other and tightly wrap the salmon pieces so the meaty sides firmly adhere to each other. Take another piece of wrap and continue to seal the package.

Place the package in a shallow dish and lay a plate or small pan on top of the salmon. Place several cans or a heavy item on top of the pan or plate to weigh down and press the fish. Place the dish in the fridge, turning the salmon over every twelve hours for 2 to 3 days. The longer the cure the drier the finished fish and more intense the flavor.

Remove the salmon from the fridge, discard all the herbs and lightly rinse. Pat dry. Using a very sharp long knife, begin slicing the salmon at a forty-five-degree angle, being sure to not cut through the skin. Serve on top of a blini, latke or bagel. A dollop of crème fraiche, sour cream or tzatziki adds a nice touch, especially when spiked with grated cucumber or dill. The salmon will hold for up to 5 days, tightly wrapped, in your fridge, but I bet it will be gobbled up long before that.

DOESN'T THAT LOOK APPETIZING

THE BIRTH OF A NEW YORK PHENOMENON

*L*ook up the word *appetizing* and you'll probably find the following definition: "adjective. appealing to the appetite, especially in appearance or aroma." That definition holds true in most of the world. However, in New York, *appetizing* takes on a whole new meaning. First, it transforms from an adjective to a noun. If there were a dictionary reserved for the language of New York, it would mean "a store that sells smoked fish and its accompanying accoutrements, sometimes along with dried fruit, nuts, candy and halvah." New York can lay claim to ownership of the appetizing store, a destination unto itself and one worthy of its iconic status.

Before the flow of Jewish immigrants to New York, this term did not exist. There were no appetizing stores in shtetls of Poland or the villages in Germany. Rather, many speculate that the word *appetizing* most likely derived from the cold appetizers (*forshpeis* in Yiddish) that families would enjoy before their main course. In a kosher home, you cannot mix dairy and meat, so the appetizer needed to be neutral, one that could be eaten with either. That would include fish, such as herring, which was prevalent in the diet of poor eastern Europeans. The word might have morphed from *appetizer* to *appetizing* to include an array of smoked fish. As Hasia Diner, author and professor of Jewish studies, noted, "Appetizing is an America institution.…Jewish immigrants who came to the United States from Lithuania or Ukraine or Belarus would have never heard of appetizing. And most foods that were sold in the appetizing, they would have never known. So this is very much an American product."

A glimpse at the appetizing counter at Russ & Daughters. *Russ & Daughters.*

The appetizing store was a destination unto itself. Immigrant New Yorkers who didn't get their food from a pushcart would make the trip to specialty stores to complete their daily shopping. Because of kosher restrictions, stores that sold meat could not sell dairy, and in turn stores that sold smoked fish and its accompaniments did not sell meat, so distinct stores developed that focused on their specific foods. There was the appetizing store, the delicatessen, the grocer, the butcher and the baker—no candlestick maker was involved in the outing. Appetizing stores fast became a Jewish immigrant phenomenon, a bridge from pushcart to proprietor, with stores propagating in every neighborhood. The appetizing store had a similar format across all boroughs. There the shopper could find an array of smoked fish and sidekicks like cream cheese and bagels. The hallmark was the appetizing counter, filled to the brim with golden smoked whitefish, loins of sturgeon, baked salmon and sable.

There were always containers of pickled herring and often pickled lox. A well-stocked store would have smoked mackerel and trout, tiny tins of caviar and, of course, the crowning glory: large slabs of smoked salmon. In many, you could buy pickles and other pickled products like sauerkraut and the famous tongue twister, pickled peppers. In addition to bagels, some featured traditional breads like fresh pumpernickel, rye and classic Russian

Strands of dried mushrooms displayed in the front window. *Photo by author.*

corn bread. There were baked goods as well: babkas and rugelach and challah for Shabbat dinner. No appetizing store was complete without a display of candies, which every *bubbe* (grandmother) had in their pocket to fend off the dreaded coughing fit. My grandmother favored those with the soft jelly filling inside and a hard candy shell. I can still picture the white wrappers with a tiny image of the fruit contained in the candy. It was an

A vintage shot of the appetizing counter and stacks of canned goods at Russ & Daughters. *Russ & Daughters.*

act of willpower to allow the candy to melt slowly in your mouth, revealing the soft center, rather than crunching down and ruining the anticipation. Alongside the candy bins, you would find all varieties of dried fruits and nuts displayed in baskets and almost always strings of dried mushrooms. A hallmark of the appetizing store was the display behind the counter. Piled high to the top of the towering shelves were cans of tuna and sardines and other conveniently packaged foods. The clerk had to risk life and limb to retrieve the items stocked behind the cash register.

The appetizing stores became a birthright, as generation after generation would take over the operation as if it were an inherited gene. At its peak, in the 1930s, there were five hundred such stores, catering mainly to a Jewish clientele. To grasp the enormity of that number, *Thrillist Magazine* in 2015 compared that roughly to the number of McDonald's and Starbucks combined operating in the city in 2015. These stores essentially bookended the city, with the most well-known and still-operating appetizing stores planted on the Lower East Side and Upper West Side as if they were giving the city a smoky embrace. As the Jewish population dwindled in some neighborhoods, so did the number of appetizing stores. However, there are still those that continue the early traditions and format and have evolved with the times as they draw customers from across all ethnicities and backgrounds. They are firmly imbedded in New York's food culture, as people continue to frequent these stores to get the finest in hand-sliced smoked fish, a selection of accompaniments that you cannot find in a supermarket and the art of *kibbitzing* (humorous banter) between customer and staff.

The GOATs (Greatest of Appetizing Trailblazers)

One of the most well-known and long-standing appetizing stores is Russ & Daughters, a Lower East Side institution that for more than one hundred years has been inextricably linked to New York's food culture. Like most immigrant stories, this story starts with the same three words: "It all began…." For Russ & Daughters, it all began in 1904, when the patriarch of the family, Joel Russ, immigrated to New York from his *shtetl* of Strzyzow, in what is now Poland. Mark Russ Federman, the founder's grandson, wrote that his grandfather came to this country, as many did, by being sponsored by a relative who had already immigrated to America. His grandfather was sponsored by his sister Channah at a cost of twenty-five dollars. He promptly began working with her selling herring that Channah procured for his pushcart. After paying his sister back, Joel opened his own business, a candy store on Myrtle Avenue in Brooklyn. After four years, he sold that business, and in 1914, his appetizing store was born. The store was originally situated on Orchard Street, but in 1920, it moved to East Houston, where it thrives today.

There was no male chauvinism in the Russ family. Joel broke the "& Sons" mold and in 1933 made his three daughters full partners, earning the distinction of the first business in this country to have an "& Daughters" in its name. For the founder's family currently running the shop, this store is much more than the sum of its parts. According to Niki Russ Federman, Mark's daughter, "it's one of New York's most unique born and bred food traditions." Federman said that you could count anywhere from twenty to thirty appetizing stores on the Lower East Side at the time they opened theirs; you could literally find an appetizing store everywhere you turned. However, of all those establishments, he believes theirs is the only one

A Lower East Side icon for more than one hundred years and counting. *Russ & Daughters.*

still operating today. That might be because of the family mantra, which Mark noted was "We're only as good as our last quarter pound of lox." He credits that *yichis* (pedigree) to the generational success of the store. Interestingly, at the time of this writing, the family and a team of television producers are conceiving a dramatic series based on Russ & Daughters.

Perhaps when this book is released, along with their other accolades, the show will have won an Emmy.

The Upper West Side, with its gargoyle-festooned, French-inspired buildings and artsy Bohemian profile, was and still is a hub of Jewish residents and influences. This accounts for the appetizing stores that have thrived on the expansive avenues that define that part of the city. Among those appetizing institutions that have stood the test of time are Barney Greengrass, Murray's Sturgeon and Zabar's. All within a stone's throw of one another, each store has its own personality and continues to attract legions of loyal fans. Let's begin with the trailblazer, Barney Greengrass, the first to establish an appetizing store. He opened in 1908 on 113th Street bordering Harlem, where there was a concentration of Jewish immigrants. A little more than twenty years later, he came downtown a bit and settled on Amsterdam Avenue at 86th Street, where the store stands today. Part of its allure might be what some consider its kitschy time capsule décor: Formica tables circa 1950s, vinyl chairs and deco-inspired black-and-white tile. Another relic of the past is its cash-only policy, so be sure to visit an ATM before going. What has kept patrons coming back is its wide variety of appetizing and its reputation for sturgeon. Barney went by the royal name the "Sturgeon King," bestowed on him by James J. Frawley, a New York politician. He traded on that moniker and is known to serve up some of the best sturgeon in the city—legendary, in fact, as even President Franklin Roosevelt was a fan. In 1939, the store shipped a batch of smoked sturgeon to him in Warm Springs, Georgia, to complete his Thanksgiving feast. That's why it is no surprise that the store received a James Beard Award as "An American Classic."

Throw a bagel up the street from Greengrass and you just might hit Murray's Sturgeon Shop on Broadway between 89th and 90th Street. Murray's is a newcomer to the block, having established itself only seventy-six years ago! The Bernstein brothers came to New York in the mid-1930s, escaping the anti-Semitic sentiment in Poland, and opened the store in 1945. The store, like so many others, was as much an appetizing store as a gathering place. In eulogizing Murray Bernstein, the store's namesake, New York real estate magnate Scott Rudin said, "He knew his product, he knew his customers. He ran a clubhouse there." His work ethic paid off, as many proclaimed, including food critic Craig Claiborne, that the store was "perhaps the finest in the city." *New York Magazine* echoed the sentiment, calling it the "Tiffany of smoked fish stores" and likening Murray's skill with a knife to that of heart surgeon Christiaan Barnard. The store has changed hands several times, but it has maintained its strict standards. What differentiates Murray's is that there is no dining room or counter stools—everything there is for takeout only.

Crane your neck out of Murray's window and with a good pair of binoculars you'll see Zabar's on the corner of Broadway and 80th. Zabar's has always had a feel of a grocery/appetizing store/delicatessen, which sets it apart from the others in the area. Its trajectory was propelled by its founder, Louis Zabar, whose story is one of determination and survival. In a recent memoir, *Zabar's*, written by Louis's late granddaughter Lori Zabar, we get a good glimpse into what makes Zabar's an iconic New York destination. Mordko Lieb Zabarka (Louis's name at birth) was raised in Ostropolia, which at that time was a Russian town northeast of Kyiv. One day, the Zabarka family heard the bootsteps of armed Cossack soldiers, who burst into their home, shot and killed his father and a sibling and wounded his mother. At his mother's urging, he made his way to New York, where he worked for a cousin in their grocery store. Louis settled in Brooklyn and married Lillian, and together in 1934 they established Zabar's. It was a wildly successful venture and quite typical until the 1960s, when everything changed. According to Geraldine Pluenneke of *Edible Manhattan*, it was in large part because they partnered with businessman and visionary Murray Klein, a colorful character to put it mildly. Klein, she said, who "once smuggled arms to what would become Israel, escaped from a Russian prison and later landed in an Italian refugee camp, began work at Zabar's sweeping floors." He can also be credited, along with Louis's two older sons Saul and Stanley, as creating the rebel of appetizing stores. Seeing the changing trends, they shifted the business model and began what they termed "deghettoizing" Jewish food. Trying to appeal to a larger demographic, they curated a store that was more than just traditional appetizing and delicatessen offerings. The result was a modern gourmet shop where they roast their own coffee, selling more than one thousand pounds a day, and feature eight hundred varieties of domestic and imported cheese, all while selling two thousand pounds of lox per day. They were among the first to feature prepared foods, now boasting more than thirty-five in-kitchen staff. This decision to diversify led to great expansion, going from its original footprint of a twenty-two-foot-wide space to one taking up nearly a full block of coveted UWS real estate, where the store attracts forty thousand customers per week.

Eli, one of Louis's sons, a third younger brother, did not follow them into the Zabar's empire, but he spread his wings and, without a passport, crossed

Zabar's has earned its place on the UWS and now occupies a full block. *Fuzheado, Wikimedia Commons.*

the great divide to the Upper East Side. He established himself with his own grocery called E.A.T. and expanded to baking bread, becoming a sit-down café, producing ice cream and artisanal candy and even curating a kitschy gift store. He was a trailblazer in providing a shop-from-home service and growing organic produce in a greenhouse atop a vintage vinegar factory. His eatery on Madison Avenue offers upscale comfort food; patrons can enjoy a hearty bowl of delicious borscht (which will set you back eighteen dollars) or a fancy caviar omelet—it is the UES, after all.

EVERYTHING OLD IS NEW AGAIN

It is no surprise that the concept of the appetizing store, with a more than one-hundred-year history, has energized new appetizing stores that are incorporating aspects of tradition with appetites of today. A fresh generation of consumers is looking for authentic experiences that combine the best of the old with new approaches. Such is decidedly the case with Shelsky's in

Left: The delicatessens of the early 1900s, such as this one owned by the father of famed cultural icon Jerome Robbins, have inspired newcomers. *NYPL Digital Collection, Jerome Robbins Dance Division.*

Below: Certainly not your typical setting for bagels and lox. Sadelle's at the Boca Raton Resort reinvents brunch for a new generation. *Author's image.*

Brooklyn. Peter Shelsky is representative of the new breed with an old soul. Even as a kid, Shelsky told me that he was reinventing typical sandwiches that he called "a party in my mouth." Look for pastrami and cured salmon with horseradish cream or smoked whitefish salad with wasabi tobiko. They pickle their own herring and lox and cure their own gravlax. When asked about who his customer is, young or old, Jewish or not, he plainly explained, "I'm selling nostalgia, but it's tasty nostalgia and all the foodies who didn't even grow up eating this food feels it's awesome stuff."

If you want your appetizing in a very appetizing space, then Sadelle's is your stop. It has reinvented the bagel and lox experience, calling itself "a modern ode to New York's classic tradition of all-day dining." The accolades have followed, with both *Harper's Bazaar* and *Cosmopolitan* calling it "an essential brunch destination." Its tower of smoked salmon is elegant and the surroundings posh. Think champagne and caviar-topped latkes or a classic New York combo called the LEO, made with lox, eggs and caramelized onions. These are just two of the newcomers that have taken the best of the past and reinvented them for today's generation.

~~~

Brunch Board

One of the trickiest aspects of shopping in the appetizing store is knowing how much of each item you need to buy. You don't want to run short on Nova or have expensive sturgeon left over. Lox you can freeze, but sturgeon is best eaten right after being sliced. So, this guide should help you create a host-worthy brunch board. There's an art to designing an appetizing platter. Be sure to mix colors and make everything easy to access, with spreaders handy. Have a serrated knife nearby to cut the bagels and a toaster for any of your persnickety guests. Avoid the pitfall of putting foods on the platter that just look pretty but serve no purpose, such as parsley or carrot sticks. I suggest one platter with Nova and its accoutrements and one for the smoked and pickled fish.

Here's a basic guideline to serve eight people.

- smoked salmon: 2 pounds (¼ pound per person or 2 to 3 slices/bagel)
- sturgeon: 8 slices
- kippered/baked salmon: 4 slices cut about 1½-inch thick each and then each cut in half to create 8 pieces
- sable: 8 slices
- whitefish: 2 pounds whole, carefully fileted
- assorted salads: ¼ to ½ pound per person in total—not of each salad, unless you have very hungry guests; suggested salads include whitefish, baked salmon, herring in either cream or wine sauce, chopped herring and pickled lox

An example of a well-thought-out brunch board, with all the fixings. *JudeAnd, Shutterstock.*

- caviar: Feeling fancy? It's lovely to add a small tin of your favorite caviar. I like to serve it in the tin so your guests can see the type of caviar. If you have caviar spoons, wonderful; if not, use plastic spoons, as metal will interfere with the taste. For a good savings and a great pop of color, try using red salmon caviar.
- cream cheese: select at least two varieties; generally scallion and plain cover all bases, ½ to ¾ pound each
- bagels: 1 dozen assorted
- accoutrements: thinly sliced cucumbers, thinly sliced red onion, lemon wedges and capers

IF YOU BUILD IT, THEY WILL COME

THE DELICATESSEN

*M*an and woman do not live by smoked fish alone. That could easily explain the popularity of the deli, an institution that was born in Europe, matured in America and was propelled to iconic status in New York. The delicatessen was where meat took center stage. The word *delicatessen* derived from the French word *délicatesse*, which means "delicious things." Add to that the Yiddish word *essen*, which means "to eat," and you've arrived at the perfect word for the phenomenon that sold delicious meats and fixings, proliferated every neighborhood in the early nineteenth century and changed the way New Yorkers, and the rest of the country, would eat for generations.

The concept of the delicatessen—whether in Germany selling cured meats, Italy at a local salumeria or in France, where it was known as charcuterie—has been part of European culture for eons. It's no surprise then that the first delis in America were opened by those same immigrants when they arrived in America. Germans, both Jewish and non-Jewish, and those from the Alsace-Lorraine region of France established shops. Jane Ziegelman in her book *97 Orchard* cited the very first purveyor of delicatessen items as Paul Gabel, who arrived in 1848 from Germany. He stocked everything from sausages and cheese to sweets and breads. He was labeled by the *New York Tribune* as a "delicatessen handler." Ted Merwin, author of *Pastrami on Rye*, wrote that the first delis were selling "blood sausage from Italy, pigs' knuckles from France, air-dried beef from Spain." He went on to note that even in Chinatown, delicatessens were springing up. Andrew

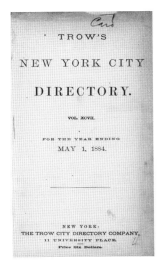

TROW'S

NEW YORK CITY

DIRECTORY.

VOL. XCVII.

FOR THE YEAR ENDING
MAY 1, 1884.

NEW YORK:
THE TROW CITY DIRECTORY COMPANY,
11 UNIVERSITY PLACE.
Price Six Dollars.

Trow's, published since 1786, was a directory reflecting businesses through the boroughs of New York. *NYPL, Irma and Paul Milstein Division of United States History, Local History and Genealogy.*

F. Smith wrote that delicatessens "filled the gap between butcher shops and grocery stores." By the 1890s, the LES was filled with stores like Gabel's. These were essentially grocers; many were not kosher, but they were the forerunners of the Jewish deli, which was closely modeled on German counterparts.

In 1884, *Trow's New York Business Directory*, listed "Delicatessens" between "deeds" and "Dental Equipment." This was its first business-related mention. Surprisingly, at this point in time, the Jewish deli was not yet a thing. While the Tenth Ward, an area of the LES a little more than one hundred acres, was home to a concentration of Jewish immigrants, a survey done at the turn of the century noted that there were fifty confectionery stores but only ten delicatessens. Additionally, as Merwin cited, "in the entire immigrant ghetto, there were more than 1000 kosher butcher shops, selling an impressive six hundred thousand pounds of kosher beef a week." Even in the cramped tenements, the kitchens were central to the apartment and the hub of the home. Women would buy meat from the kosher butcher and pickle or cure them at home. That would all change in just a few years.

The Jewish delicatessen in its initial stages in America reflected its neighborhood and the needs of its patrons. For many, the delicatessen was an opportunity to enjoy a greater variety of foods and offered new, affordable, convenient offerings for the underserved immigrant. As Deborah Dash Moore noted in *Jewish New York*, "Delis became such an iconic New York Jewish institution that their presence often identified a Jewish neighborhood more clearly even that that of a synagogue."

Despite their different offerings, Ziegelman noted that the non-Jewish German and Jewish delis were "on a parallel track" when it came to décor and setup. "The delicatessen's main staging area was a white marble counter, where the meats were displayed and sliced for the customer. The salads were arrayed in a row of stoneware crocks." Not only was the décor consistent throughout the various delis that were popping up, but the attire was as well. The deli, with its fat filled meats and sawdust floors, needed to combat the

A reproduction of a typical kitchen at 97 Orchard Street, now home to the Tenement Museum. *Carol M. Highsmith, Wikimedia Commons.*

naysayers who felt that this type of "fast food" was a scourge on society, so they needed to project an image of cleanliness. An article from the *Mogen David Delicatessen Magazine*—that's right, the deli had its own publication—reported that anyone handling or serving food was "compelled" to wear white (think hospital garb lab coat). This sanitized dress code extended even to head coverings, as any deli man worth his slicer wore a white paper hat as well. The magazine reported on the various issues related to the delicatessen and published a fair pricing guide as well.

The question remained whether the shop was a deli or a restaurant, as there is a fine line between the two. A deli sold the products that, when combined, become a sandwich or a meal, while a restaurant served prepared entrées. Additionally, the original delis were counter service only, while restaurants featured sit-down dining. As delis evolved, they began to add seating. Not only did having tables increase the profitability, but it was also a practical way to get around the blue laws. These rules forbade serving take-out food after 10:00 a.m. on Sundays. Because most Jewish delis were also closed on

Left: The *Mogen David* was the industry magazine regulating and reporting on the delicatessen. *NYPL, Digital Collection, Dorot Jewish Division.*

Right: The fair price list dictated what a delicatessen could charge for their various offerings. *NYPL, Digital Collection, Dorot Jewish Division.*

Saturdays for the Jewish Sabbath, they essentially lost an entire weekend of business. An 1895 article in the *New York Times* reported on a ruling by Judge Allison with regard to a delicatessen owner arrested and released "for selling sausage on Sunday." Acting Chief of Police Conlon had this to say:

> *I understand the indictment was dismissed because the evidence was weak. If they [delicatessens] sell any prepared food, it must be consumed in the place. If they sell goods to be taken away after 10 o'clock, they will be arrested for violating the Sunday law. Section 267 of the Penal Code is very plain and covers the point.*

Hence, out of practical necessity, in many instances, the deli morphed into a restaurant with sit down seating to legally serve prepared foods. Merwin pointed to a 1910 lawsuit in which one business owner sued another over the fact that they had tables, which made them a restaurant, not a deli. The judge decreed that "delicatessens come in all types comparing them 'in their

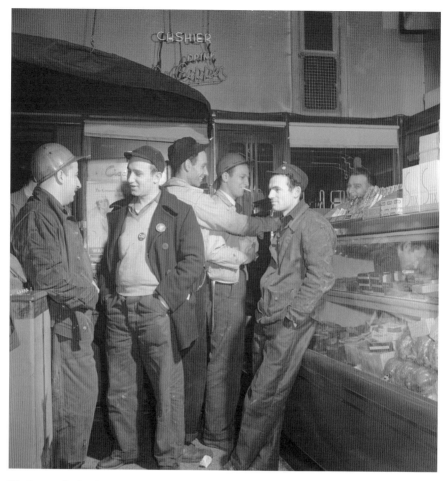

Workers gathering in a deli. *Marjory Collins, photographer, Library of Congress, Prints and Photographs Division.*

infinite variety' to Cleopatra." There were also different deli options. As the deli proliferated, you could find kosher delis that served only kosher-certified meats and accompaniments, and no dairy products, so no Swiss on your corned beef sandwich. There were delis that served both meat and dairy but adhering to Jewish food preferences, rendering them non-kosher. These were euphemistically called "kosher style." This gave way to the tradition of blazing neon signs on the store exterior so the deli could draw attention not only to the name but also its status as either kosher or non-kosher, as well as to establish provenance regarding who was providing the meat. Then there were those that served only dairy. There will be a quiz at the end!

In 1903, Hasia Diner wrote that the *Jewish Daily Forward* created a new Yiddish word for a phenomenon it was observing. It coined the term *oyesessen*, meaning "eating out," and declared that "oyesessen is spreading every day, especially in New York." This began the Jewish delicatessen era. The deli became more than a place to grab a bite or buy a half pound of salami. It became the therapist's office, your lifeline to news from back home, a cultural haven for poets and writers, a debate club and a social hall. The Irish had their pubs and the Italian community its social clubs. The deli served both purposes for Jewish immigrant New Yorkers. It provided a place where they could gather and speak to one another in Yiddish without judgement or fear of being viewed as outsiders.

The deli was also a gathering place for the young new Americans. Ziegelman described the hordes of kids in the 1900s leaving their school "for a deli lunch, of pickles and halvah." For many, it was their weekend hangout. In his memoir, *A Walker in the City*, Alfred Kazin wrote, "Saturday at twilight, neighborhood kids haunted the local delicatessen, waiting for it to reopen. As soon as it did, the kids raced in." As time went on, some delis chose to stay open on Saturdays. My father, the son of immigrants, born in 1926 in the Bronx, shared with me one of his recollections of how he spent his Saturdays. He explained that was movie day, as he and his buddies would pool together a dollar to go to the local deli called Schweller's on Jerome Avenue. He said that the "fragrance of walking in there still stays with me with barrels of pickles and sauerkraut brining." There they would buy hot dogs to bring to the movie theater and "eat them under the watchful eye of a matron, dressed in white, whose job was to supervise the unattended minors in the theater." This ritual was replicated thousands of times for this generation of kids growing up in New York. The deli eventually became a place that mirrored the attitudes and aspirations of these first-generation Americans. As Merwin wrote, "The history of the delicatessen is the history of Jews eating themselves into Americans."

The Legends

With the advent of the deli, as Hasia Diner noted, "The formerly poor started to eat blintzes, kreplach, kasha-varnitchkes [*sic*], strudel, noodles, knishes and more importantly, meat every day." By the 1970s, there were more than five thousand delicatessens across New York City that would attest to that trend. However, eating habits have changed over the last few decades.

Gone are the days of the deli being a social hub and eating there daily, as once was the habit. Neighborhoods have changed, in some cases with the Jewish population moving out to the suburbs and new food traditions moving in. The food landscape has changed, and the great institution that was the New York deli has changed with it. Happily, there are still some legends standing, and they deserve our attention; a few that are gone should be noted in memoriam.

Katz's is perhaps the most recognizable New York deli; it has gone from a neighborhood eatery to a destination. According to David Sax's *Save the Deli*, it is the oldest Jewish deli in the world. Katz's hasn't changed very much since it opened on New York's Lower East Side. It began in 1888 and was known as Iceland Brothers, located on Ludlow Street. When Willy Katz joined in 1903, the name changed to Iceland & Katz. The name Katz's was formally cemented in 1910 when Willy's cousin bought out their partners and formed Katz's Delicatessen. In 1917, it moved across the street to its current location on Houston. That's when its now famous slogan, "Katz's, that's all," was painted on the building's exterior. It seems that the sign painter took Willy literally—when asked, "What should the sign say?" Willy replied, "Katz's, that's all," and so that's what he painted!

Another well-known sign at Katz's reads, "Hope you have what she had" as an homage to the scene from *When Harry Met Sally*. You might recall Meg Ryan's oohing and aahing in mocking Billy Crystal and then the iconic line delivered by Rob Reiner's mother, "I'll have what she's having." Yup, that scene was filmed at Katz's. In the restaurant, you can sit beneath the sign that points to the exact table from the film. On a recent visit, I asked a gentleman from Virginia why he was coming to Katz's. He said because it was famous. When I asked what for, he quickly replied, *"Harry Met Sally."* I told him it should be more about its pastrami and corned beef, neither of which he had ever tasted before. I gave him a short spiel on Katz's, and then he replied, "Now I'm here to eat my way through history." When I asked what brought a French family behind us on line to Katz's, they simply answered, "Reputation." Its reputation is solidly built on quality food, mile-high sandwiches, a kosher-style approach and a more than century-old ordering process. No QR codes here. When you reach the front of the line, you receive a small yellow ticket, used to record everything you purchase. The chit is then surrendered at the exit as you leave satiated and significantly poorer. Be sure not to lose the ticket, as if you do there is a fifty-dollar penalty charge! I asked the affable greeter/bouncer/ticket taker if they really do collect a lost ticket fee, and he told me with a bit of a grin, "We do everything

A shot of Katz's Deli showing the famous signage and lines trailing down the block. *Photo by author.*

we can to try and help the customer find it, but every day at least two to three people do pay the penalty."

The counterman is integral to the Katz's experience. As the line queues up, you file behind a cutter numbered from one to eight and patiently wait your turn. The cutter will slip you a taste of meat to sample, and then, with a swift blade that would leave Zorro in its wake, he slices everything for your sandwich by hand. The custom is to tip this counterman much as you would leave a dollar or two in a church collection plate. I have a very personal recollection of one of my early visits to Katz's, a rite of passage for every New Yorker. As my sister and I waited in the car, our mother entered Katz's, collected her meal ticket and presented it to

Controlled chaos as you queue up to place your order at Katz's Deli, priceless chit in hand. *Author's image.*

the counterman. He sliced her several tastes of fatty corned beef, her favorite. My mother, unfamiliar with the gratuity expectation, failed to tip the counterman and was escorted out the door, without her sandwich. Watching her hurried exit, we quickly whisked her away. If you want to get in on the action, come on a weekday, as tourists and New Yorkers alike flood the restaurant on weekends. Be sure to have a few singles handy to tip your counterman—or a running getaway car.

Another deli with an epic history is the 2nd Avenue Deli, a New York institution since 1954. The restaurant was made legendary not only because of its wide array of kosher specialties or location on what became known as "Knish Alley" on the Yiddish rialto, but also because of its engaging and vibrant owner, Abe Lebewohl. Sax lovingly described Abe as climbing the ladder from soda jerk on Coney Island to owner of a ten-seat luncheonette, after which Lebewohl put 2nd Avenue Deli on the map of Gotham institutions. A daily lineup of limousines could be seen outside the 2nd Avenue Deli, waiting to bring sandwiches to hungry Wall Street bankers. He was not just

The 2nd Avenue Deli's 1974 menu cover, showing the throngs of people who would congregate in the area when the restaurant first opened. *NYPL, Digital Collection, Rare Book Division.*

a deli man through and through, he was also a lifeline to New York's poor and hungry. Sax wrote, "Any time the many homeless from the neighborhood came into the 2nd Ave. Deli, Abe made sure they left full. Then he would pack up the day's leftovers into the delivery truck and take it to shelters around town." Abe's daughter told Sax that he was known to leave the truck unlocked at night so one particular homeless man could take shelter there until morning. His story is the stuff of docudramas. On March 4, 1996, Abe Lebewohl was robbed and murdered as he brought the previous night's receipts to the bank. The *New York Times* reporting on the murder said that he was shot just six blocks from the restaurant. No suspects were identified, and the murder remains unsolved. His death stunned the city, and hordes of people attended his funeral, culminating in a distraught rabbi collapsing on the street. Lebewohl reminded us of what it took to be an immigrant entrepreneur and bring good food and good cheer to a city. After a brief closing, the deli reopened under the ownership of two of his nephews, who longed to carry on the traditions Abe established.

Gone but Not Forgotten

In 2012, the famed Stage Deli closed, and four years later, its neighbor, Carnegie Deli, followed suit. These two institutions were the poster children for glamorizing the deli. The Stage opened in 1937 and enjoyed a seventy-five-year run two blocks from Carnegie Hall. I suppose they got there through practice, practice, practice. The deli was started by Max Asnes, a Russian immigrant. It featured sandwiches named for Broadway shows and a star-studded following, including celebrities like Adam Sandler and baseball legend Mickey Mantle, who in the 1950s lived above the restaurant. The *New York Times* reported in 1978 that regulars Muhammad Ali and Joe Frazier "always eat the same corned beef and cream cheese on rye sandwiches." It was said

Left: Stage Deli's menu cover from 1968. Notice Max in the upper-left corner and the caricatures depicting staff and clientele. *NYPL, Digital Collection, Rare Book Division.*

Right: Carnegie Deli's menu featured the key characters at the restaurant and the neighborhood landmarks. *NYPL, Digital Collection, Rare Book Division.*

that the Stage Deli was where "celebrities go to look at people." Max Asnes of the Stage would annually host a matzo ball contest, where judges analyzed the size and shape of the perfect matzo ball. This became a New York City tradition that was irreplaceable when the deli closed.

Carnegie celebrated eighty years in the neighborhood. While it changed hands a few times, the deli garnered its true position as one of New York's best under the ownership of Leo Steiner and Milton Parker. Steiner was known to work the crowds much like a standup comedian works the room. He was credited with creating a sixty-pound Statue of Liberty carved from chopped liver and was tapped to feed the international attendees at a 1983 G7 Summit held in Virginia. Parker exceled behind the scenes, and according to its website, he was dubbed "CPM," Corned Beef and Pastrami Maven. It, too, garnered a celebrity following, which revolved around television writers such as Mel Brooks and Carl Reiner. The restaurant, known for its skyscraper sandwiches, was quoted as saying, "If you can finish your meal, we've done something wrong." Its manager, Sandy Levine, had an infamous reputation, culminating in a *New York Post* headline calling him the "Shyster of Smoked Meats." Its closing left a void in the area and signaled the end of an era.

The Show Must Go On

The attraction and longevity of the New York deli had as much to do with its cast of characters as it did the food. There is a reason why the Jewish deli so firmly imprinted on New York's collective food memory. From the moment you entered the deli, you were transported to a Broadway show. The outside signs were flashing in neon, with the store's name and provenance of where its meats came from. The countermen were dressed in garb reserved for their role, and as if out of central casting, they tended to be curt and have a limited speaking part. The waiters, on the other hand, were given the best lines, spewing menu advice, tossing around insults and creating an obnoxious character reminiscent of a Parisienne bistro waiter who pays little attention to the customer's wants and needs. Ask for a non-bent fork or an unchipped soup bowl and the snooty waiter would give you a death ray stare. Then, to ease the tension, the affable restaurant owner entered in Act 2, with a personality bathed in the ability to *kibbitz*, *schmooze* (make light conversation) and make you feel as if you are enjoying that bowl of matzo bowl soup in your own kitchen. The customer played a part as well. They might cast a young immigrant finding his way up the ladder, with a bearded face and a Yiddish accent, or it could be an up-and-coming actor catching a bite after a show on 2nd Avenue. Every character had a part in creating the perfect scene, well choreographed with precise timing, plenty of mood lighting, notable set design, familiar costuming and the feeling when it was over that everyone was satisfied and the performance went well. Unfortunately, the curtain has come down on the deli in many ways, but new and exciting versions are popping up. As Broadway revivals go, they are not always the same as the original, but they offer new perspectives for a new audience.

Funny, You Don't Look Newish

Normally, an institution that's been around for fifty-plus years can't be called a "newcomer," but because of the history of some of the New York delis, these new kids on the block will have to endure the label. They have kept much of what made the old-school delis famous, perhaps with a bit less *shtick*. This would include delis like Sarge's on the UES, where all the meats are cured on the premises and the blintzes are homemade, or Riverdale's kosher deli Liebman's, which some call the "Katz's of the Bronx." Another

New York favorite is Pastrami Queen. This monarchy of pastrami opened in 1956 in Brooklyn, then moved to Queens and now calls both the UES and UWS home. It has earned its royal title, as even the late great Anthony Bourdain dubbed it the "quintessential New York meal."

There are delis that have a history rooted in New York but unusual ancestry, such as David's Brisket House. Riyadh Gazali along with his brother Farouq are the current owners of this Bed-Stuy Brooklyn institution. Their backstory is a New York story. Their uncle, a Muslim Yemini immigrant, was formerly in business with a Jewish Yemini partner. Across the street from the shop they operated stood David's Brisket House, owned and operated by a Russian Jew. The Yemini partners bought the shop and merged their business with David's. When the Jewish partner died, the uncle continued to manage the brisket house, eventually passing it on to his nephews. When I asked how and why they maintain the Jewish traditions that David started, Riyadh answered, "We inherited the business, and we didn't want to change anything out of respect for the history of the Jewish culture." This brisket house, also known for pastrami and corned beef, is a great example of the merging of cultures and the concept of honoring tradition. As Riyadh told me, Jewish and Muslim communities have always lived side by side, as do brisket and the city. He says, "They are both part of the culture, the two go hand in hand."

There is additionally a rebirth of old-school delis, doing things in new-school ways. They are fueled by those who use the traditions of the past to inform the taste buds of the future. Mile End in Brooklyn comes to mind, where Montreal smoked meats mingle with tradition; this deli, barely out of its teens, draws crowds every day. You can enjoy twists on the classics like house-cured smoked meat hash or Bubbie's brisket with JewBQ. If you want a swanky cocktail with your pastrami deviled egg or the feel of a speakeasy as you easily devour your smoked tongue slider, then head upstairs from the 2nd Avenue Deli for a nostalgic turn of old New York. 2nd Avenue Bar & Essen is bringing back the Lansky days, without the plotting or racketeering. These restaurateurs are not iconoclasts, but rather trendsetters for the reinvention of the iconic New York delicatessen. Skip the mini mart if you want a true deli experience. Look for those that smoke their own meat, prepare their own salads and carry on the traditions that set the standards.

Kasha Varnishkes

(Reprinted with permission from Recipes Remembered: A Celebration of Survival, *June Hersh, Ruder Finn Press, May 2011.)*

Every New York deli had traditional Ashkenazi dishes that transported diners back to their hometown. One that still remains a favorite is kasha varnishkes. Eastern European cooks know that when you combine the goodness of whole grain buckwheat groats with slowly sautéed onions, you get a dish that can be enjoyed hot or cold, on its own or as part of a well-rounded meal. It's never been trendy, but it sure is good.

Toasted buckwheat groats and caramelized onions sounds much trendier than kasha varnishkes. *Tjingko, Wikimedia Commons.*

Yields 6 to 8 servings.

12 ounces uncooked bowtie pasta
3 tablespoons vegetable oil or butter
2 large yellow onions, chopped, about 2 cups
1 egg beaten
1 cup kasha
2 cups broth (beef, chicken or vegetable)
Kosher salt and pepper

Bring a large pot of salted water to boil and cook the noodles according to package directions; drain and reserve.

While the pasta cooks, heat the oil or butter in a large skillet and cook and stir the onions over medium heat until they are very brown but not burned, 20–30 minutes; using a slotted spoon, remove the onions from the pan and set aside.

In a small bowl, mix the egg and kasha. Using the same pan, spread the kasha and egg mixture in a thin layer and cook, over medium heat, until the egg has cooked out and the kasha lightly browns, about 3 minutes.

In a small saucepan, bring the broth to a boil. Slowly pour the hot broth into the skillet with the kasha. Stir to completely break up any bits and simmer covered for 15 minutes. Check for tenderness, as they could need another few minutes. Add the reserved noodles and onions to the skillet and season to taste with salt and pepper. If the mixture seems dry, add a bit more oil or butter or a little more broth.

A CUT ABOVE

THE MEATS

EARL WHO?

Jewish people have had a love affair with the sandwich long before the noble namesake Earl of Sandwich devoured one during a card game in the 1700s. According to Ted Merwin, the first sandwich can be traced to Hillel the Elder not at the turn of the century, but rather at the turn of the first millennium, during the time of King Herod and Emperor Augustus of Rome. He fulfilled a commandment to eat both matzo and bitter herbs to commemorate the Jews' freedom from enslavement in Egypt. Hillel wrapped herbs and shredded lamb in what most assume was a soft version of matzo, more like a pita or roti. He called this folded handheld creation *korech*, based on the ancient Hebrew word *lekarech*, which means to encircle or envelop. Not to minimize the many scholarly teachings of Hillel, but creating the first sandwich could just be one of the best legacies he passed down. Flash forward to the late 1800s in New York City, where the sandwich was not just reinvented but elevated to iconic status. Calling one of the overstuffed, meat-packed sandwiches that you need to unhinge your jaw to take a bite from "iconic" just might make a sandwich blush. It became a conveyance to devour the meats that spiced up New York's tastebuds. If the delicatessen was the tabernacle, then these meats were the high priests.

SPARRING PARTNERS

In the New York delicatessen, there is a long-standing matchup between pastrami and corned beef as to which meat is more popular. In one steamer we have pastrami, fatty and juicy with a spicy, smokey flavor and a Romanian lineage. It is usually cut from the navel, with fat in every layer. It's prepped for battle with a rigorous regimen of brining, curing, smoking and steaming. It has a strong jab, and for some, it hits below the belt after eating. In the other steamer there's corned beef, with an Irish pedigree and a lightly pickled taste. It comes in thin and lean, with a pale pink complexion; when piled high on a sandwich, especially paired with kraut and Russian dressing, it packs a powerful punch. After more than a century of these two sparring, we have a split decision. This pair has joined the pantheon of duos that put the New York deli on the map, and both have earned their place as iconic New York foods. In his book *A Lost Paradise: Early Reminiscences*, Samuel Chitzinoff shared experiences from his family deli in the early 1900s, when a tin clothes boiler was used to cook pastrami and corned beef. He described "the fatty bubbling water spilled on the floor, and the delicious aggressive aroma of superheated pickled beef would mingle with and soon overpower the prevailing insistent, native, musty, dank smell." Today, pastrami and corned beef are a dynamic duo, living harmoniously side by side in a more congenial deli steamer. It's a mouthwatering ritual to watch the counterman plunge the long fork into the bubbly bath and bring out a glistening slab ready to slice. The counterman gets a pickled facial, and you get a juicy piece of meat.

Meat Pastrami, the Current Frontrunner

In the contest of iconic New York deli meats, pastrami would be the winner, but not by a knockout. It is the specialty that has launched delis to stardom and has diners lining up around the block. It has a long history, but it truly reached its destiny when it arrived in New York. A version of pastrami can be traced to the fourteenth century, when meat was dried by pressing out its juices (think jerky before a dehydrator was invented). According to Merwin, "Turkish horsemen in Central Asia preserved meat by inserting it in the sides of their saddles, where their legs would press against it as they rode; the meat was tenderized in the animal's sweat." Yum! The word for pastrami derived from Romanian, Russian, Turkish and Armenian words such as *pastra*, *pastromá*, *pastirma* and *basturma*, meaning meat that was pressed. While this true Romanian version was not the thick, unctuous slices we enjoy today, can we assume that this tradition of preparing pastrami arrived in New York with the Romanian immigrants as they settled into tenements on the Lower East Side. How pastrami found a home in the deli showcase might sound like the stuff of fables, but Patricia Volk, in her memoir *Stuffed*, assured us that it's true. She wrote of her paternal grandfather Sussman Volk:

> *Having failed to make it as a tinker, Volk left the cookware business in 1887 and opened a butcher shop on Delancey Street. A friend asked Volk to store a suitcase in the basement while he returned home to Romania for a visit. In return, he gave Volk his pastrami recipe, which Volk used to such success that he had to open a delicatessen to meet the demand.*

There has been, according to Merwin, corroboration of this story, and he noted that "at the turn of the twentieth century, Romanian delicatessen stores appeared with their goose-pastrama." That's right, perhaps the first real mention of pastrami in a New York deli was not beef but *goose*. It has been noted that in the 1890s, this meat was referred to as "pastrama"; by the 1900s, it was called "pastrame," and after World War II it was "pastrami." The difference in spellings could be the difference in the meats used—that is something we might never have a clear answer for. What seems to be clear is that while goose pastrami was a Romanian specialty, substituting beef for goose was a New York concept.

However, like all good food stories, there's another possibility that's been floated. *The Forward* reported on research by Daniel Vaughn, the barbecue editor of *Texas Monthly*, who "found ads for a Corpus Christi Jewish butcher shop selling 'pastromie' in 1916." This doesn't predate Volk's story, but it does call into question if the beef pastrami we enjoy today might have actually started out in Texas and found its way to New York. Vaughn makes a good case for this, saying that "Czech and German butchers brought their meat-preserving processes to Texas…and then made their way to the east coast." So the next time you order a pastrami sandwich, you could engage a Texas drawl. Not so fast, says Andrew Silverstein, who did the sleuthing for an article in *The Forward*. He maintains that references to New York smoked meats date back to 1894, citing an ad that appeared in the Yiddish publication *Fraye Arbayter Shtime* (*Free Voice of Labor*): "B. Meiers is the only manufacturer of the world-famous pastrama. Only he knows the code of how it is perfected and all the other pastramas are just imitations." Silverstein

Left: This slab of pastrami came straight out of the steamer, ready to be sliced. *Photo by author.*

Below: Goose pastrami, the forerunner of the beef version we eat today. ©*Holly A. Heyser, 2022, photo.hollyheyser.com.*

points to this ad to refute and debunk the notion that Texas pastrami predates New York. However, the question beckons: was the ad talking about beef pastrami or goose? While the origin of actual beef pastrami as we know it today is cloudy, we just need to be grateful to whomever it was who thought to take a century-old Romanian dehydrated version, apply it to goose meat and morph it into the beef pastrami that New York made famous.

No matter who can take credit for its origin, New York beef pastrami has gone on to achieve iconic status in part because the way it was prepared here was different than previous iterations of the same meat. Food journalist R.W. Apple once wrote that "all other varieties, to tell the truth, pale in comparison with the moist, garlicky stuff Jewish immigrants brought with them to New York from central and eastern Europe." As the owner of Katz's, the house that pastrami built, Jake Dell estimates that they sell between twenty thousand to thirty thousand pounds of pastrami in a typical week. To solidify its importance in pop culture, pastrami made a curious guest appearance on the final season of *Seinfeld*. George decided to combine his love for a pastrami sandwich with his more carnal instincts and began consuming both at the same time. Let's just say it didn't go well for his relationship with his girlfriend, but he and the pastrami sandwich were still going strong in the end.

The Contender

Corned beef is no slouch, and for many, it does not take a backseat to pastrami. Katz's deli notes that for its first century, corned beef was twice as popular as pastrami. The custom of eating pickled meats such as corned beef dates to biblical times; according to Merwin, the Hebrews would eat roasted meat during a holy feast. They then asked the priests if they could consume this "joyful" delight at other times, and the priests decreed that they could under one condition: the meat would have to be pickled for two days, presumably to make it less joyful. Unlike pastrami, corned beef is pickled and gained true popularity in northern Europe. The city of Cork, Ireland, was home to the center of corned beef trade somewhere between the seventeenth and eighteenth centuries. The first true mention of corned beef comes in a strange volume, *The Anatomy of Melancholy*, written in 1621, in which the author, Robert Burton, refers to the "corned young of an ox." Had he tried a true deli corned beef sandwich, it would have cured his melancholy and surely raised his spirits. Corned beef's presence in New

York can be traced to the influx of Irish immigrants flooding the Lower East Side. Within the tenements, it was common for cultures to mix and mingle their foodways, corned beef being one. The Irish rediscovered their love for corned beef from their Jewish neighbors. Both groups frequented the Jewish butcher to buy kosher brisket for pickling. The Jewish and Irish immigrants in New York shared more than their love for this pickled beef. *Smithsonian Magazine* pointed out that both came from hardship and experienced unrelenting discrimination, leading to a shared experience:

> *There was an understanding between the two groups, which was a comfort to the newly arriving immigrants. This <u>relationship</u> can be seen in Irish, Irish American, and Jewish-American folklore. It is not a coincidence that James Joyce made the main character of his masterpiece* Ulysses, *Leopold Bloom, a man born to Jewish and Irish parents. And, as the two Tin Pan Alley songwriters, William Jerome and Jean Schwartz write in their 1912 song* If It Wasn't for the Irish and the Jews.

The process of making corned beef is less complicated than pastrami, requiring fewer steps. The term corned beef comes from the process's large kernels of salt that resemble corn. Pickling spices such as black and red pepper, coriander, mustard seeds and bay leaves create the bath in which the brisket rests for about five days. It gets its lovely pink hue from the pink

This is an image of the Blackstone Hotel in Nebraska, built in 1916 and the most likely place the Reuben sandwich was invented. *thecottonwoodhotel.com.*

curing salt that is used. Whereas pastrami is best enjoyed in thick juicy slices with ripples of fat, most prefer their corned beef trimmed neatly and sliced thin.

Corned beef is the central ingredient in a classic New York mashup called the Reuben sandwich, a decidedly non-kosher favorite consisting of corned beef, Swiss cheese, sauerkraut and Russian dressing on toasted rye. Darwin's *On the Origin of Species* has fewer theories than how this corned beef–centric sandwich evolved. Arthur Schwartz cited one claim: "When Fern Snider, a waitress from the Blackstone Hotel in Omaha, Nebraska, entered the recipe in a contest and won a national sandwich competition…she knew about the sandwich because it was on the menu at her hotel." According to this version, a local grocer named Reuben Kulakofsky developed the sandwich to feed his buddies at a poker game, sometime between 1922 and 1925. It was such a hit that they named it for him and put it on the menu. But wait, another version as told by Elizabeth Weil in her article "Who Really Invented the Reuben," credits her great-grandfather for inventing the sandwich. She says that in the 1920s, her great-grandfather, who oversaw the kitchen at the Blackstone Hotel in Nebraska, created the sandwich *for* (not by) Reuben Kulakofsky, who was playing poker there that evening. He incorporated the ingredients and added the finishing touch to a perfect Reuben: a hot press. The story then goes on to credit Fern for bringing it to a wider audience. But wait, there's one more story about an accountant named William Hamerly, who is said to have concocted the sandwich and named it for restaurateur Arnold Reuben to honor his charitable work. So, let's check the scores; that's two involving Reuben Kulakofsky, albeit with varying recollections, and one for Arnold Reuben. Either way, it's a New York classic.

More than Meats the Eye: Tongue and Brisket

If pastrami and corned beef were the headliners, tongue and brisket were the well-received supporting players. While you might not give them true iconic status, they deserve an honorary mention as other popular offerings in the New York deli. Brisket is closely related to corned beef, as they both come from the brisket of the cow. It was an economical and kosher cut of meat for *shtetl* (small village) dwellers in eastern Europe. Brisket became associated with Jewish holidays and would be braised for long periods of time to render the meat tender and juicy. Delis serve it up on sandwiches; however, it often stands alone as a main course, with no bread needed. Smothered in gravy,

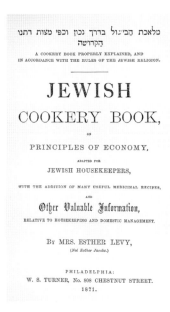

מלאכת הבישול בדרך נכון וכפי מצות רתנו
הקדושה

A COOKERY BOOK PROPERLY EXPLAINED, AND
IN ACCORDANCE WITH THE RULES OF THE JEWISH RELIGION.

JEWISH
COOKERY BOOK,
OR
PRINCIPLES OF ECONOMY,
ADAPTED FOR
JEWISH HOUSEKEEPERS,
WITH THE ADDITION OF MANY USEFUL MEDICINAL RECIPES,
AND
Other Valuable Information,
RELATIVE TO HOUSEKEEPING AND DOMESTIC MANAGEMENT.

BY MRS. ESTHER LEVY,
(Née Esther Jacobs.)

PHILADELPHIA:
W. S. TURNER, No. 808 CHESTNUT STREET.
1871.

The cover of Esther Levy's cookbook, printed in 1871, with the longest title ever. *Photo by author.*

topped with onions or potted with veggies, brisket is a classic deli entrée.

For some, just the thought of eating tongue sounds awful, but it's actually offal. Offal, also known as variety meats (doesn't *that* sound better?), finds its place alongside sweetbreads or calves' liver as those dishes you hate to love or love to hate. Tongue gained popularity in eastern Europe, as it was an inexpensive cut and particularly juicy due to its very high fat content. It developed a following that followed it to New York and became a choice deli meat, selling at a whopping twenty-five cents more per pound than other meats. The first Jewish cookbook in America and the one with the longest title was *Mrs. Esther Levy's Jewish Cookery Book on Principles of Economy Adapted for Jewish Housekeepers with Medical Recipes and Other Valuable Information Relative to Housekeeping and Domestic Management* (whew!). Written in 1871, her cookbook covered everything from "Observations on Pickles" to a number of recipes focused on tongue, suggesting that it was already a popular dish to prepare at home, often for Sukkot. It's especially delicious when paired on a sandwich with corned beef or served polonaise style, with a sweet raisin-spiked sauce. It should be tried at least once.

~~~

Mash-Up Hash-Up Latkes

These latkes are a mashup of leftover deli meat and a traditional latke recipe, perfect for a breakfast hash or a delicious lunch or side dish.

2 russet potatoes, peeled and cut in half lengthwise
1 medium onion, peeled and halved
2 eggs
½ pound leftover corned beef/pastrami, roughly chopped (about 1 cup)
¼ cup matzo meal

1 teaspoon baking powder
1–2 tablespoons all-purpose flour
Oil for frying

No fancy gadgets needed—use a *küchenreibe*, German for kitchen grater, to prepare latkes. *Wikimedia Commons.*

To easily grate the potatoes, use a food processor with the shredding disc. Alternatively, you can use a box grater, but watch your knuckles! Shred the potatoes, followed by the onion. Place the mixture in a dish towel and wring to remove the excess liquid.

Place the dry potatoes and onions in a medium mixing bowl. Stir in the eggs until thoroughly combined and then mix in the chopped meats. Stir in the matzo meal and baking powder and work it through with your hands to see if the mixture holds together. If it does not, add flour until the mixture can hold its shape when rolled into a ball.

In a large skillet, heat ¼ inch neutral oil over medium to medium-high heat until shimmering. Test it for temperature by dropping a piece of shredded potato into the oil. If it quickly browns, the oil is ready.

Roll the mixture into a ball a bit large than a golf ball and place in the pan, allowing enough room for the latkes to be pressed flat with the spatula.

Fry 3–4 minutes, or until the underside is browned; flip and continue cooking until both sides are brown and crispy. Remove with a slotted spatula to a paper towel and allow to drain.

Continue frying until all the mixture is used. Serve hot with a mixture of equal parts mayo and BBQ sauce on the side; for a non-kosher presentation, combine equal parts sour cream and spicy brown mustard.

A flyer depicting immigrants coming to America. The Hebrew translates to "Food will win the war—You came here seeking freedom, now you must help to preserve it—Wheat is needed for the allies—Waste nothing." *Library of Congress.*

The bustling streets of the Lower East Side, circa 1900s. *Library of Congress, Prints and Photographs Division.*

Mouthwatering plate of bite-sized pushcart puppies (recipe on pages 25–26), alongside a good old burger. *Ben Fink Photography, reprinted from* The Kosher Carnivore.

Above: Central Park, 5th Avenue—the intersection of hungry New Yorkers and food carts. *Tomas Fano, Wikimedia Commons.*

Left: Showing the bagel the love it deserves. January 15 is National Bagel Day. *Sergey Meshkov, Pexels.com.*

The colorful rainbow bagel delights young and old. *Caitlin Wilson, @lillynwilson.*

This record-breaking bagel with lox and all the fixings needed a saw to be cut! *Courtesy of Michelle Young, Untappedcities.com.*

Left: Loins of Faroe Island salmon glisten from the copious amount of salt needed to create belly lox. *Author's image.*

Below: Despite the sturgeon being taboo for some, its luscious eggs sitting atop a bagel were an indulgent luxury for others. *Jackmac34, Pixabay.*

Smoked and pickled fish with all the trimmings creates a brunch bonanza. *Russ & Daughters.*

The finest appetizing stores always had a beautiful array of dried fruit, nuts and candy. *Ingrid Prats, Shutterstock.*

Above: When you can't decide between corned beef or pastrami at Katz's, order both— just be sure that yellow chit stays with you at all times. *Author's image.*

Left: Did the movie *When Harry Met Sally* make Katz's famous, or did Katz's immortalize the movie? You can sit where it all took place. *Erik39, Wikimedia Commons.*

Top: A thing of beauty: a perfectly prepared Reuben sandwich. *Rebecca, Adobe Stock.*

Bottom: Nothing cozies up to brisket like a bowl of kasha varnishkes. *Ben Fink Photography, reprinted from* The Kosher Carnivore.

Left: A slab of pastrami straight from the steamer ensures a juicy sandwich. *Author's image.*

Below: **GBD** (golden brown delicious) latkes are made even more so when stuffed with pastrami and corned beef and topped with a spicy mayo. *Author's image.*

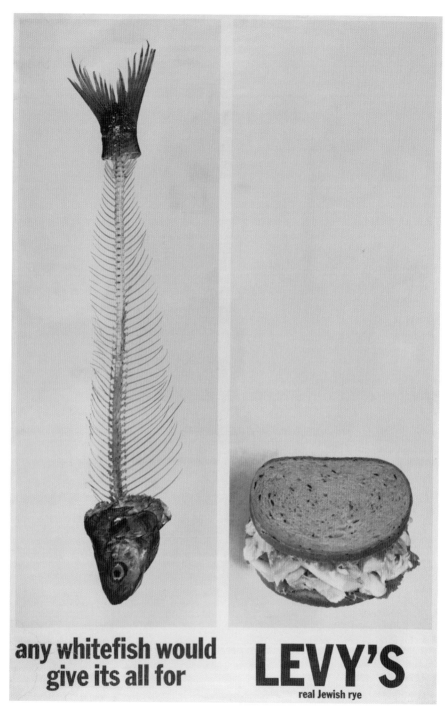

any whitefish would give its all for **LEVY'S** real Jewish rye

This clever 1962 Levy's rye bread ad says it all. *Library of Congress, Prints and Photographs Division.*

Top: Resourceful and frugal eastern European cooks used leftover matzo to make delicious matzo balls. *Natalie Hanin, Adobe Stock.*

Bottom: Crisp and fresh half-sour pickles, swimming happily in their brine at the Pickle Guys. *Author's image.*

The blintz is the perfect sweet bite and conveyance of almost any topping. *Nate Bailey, Flickr.*

Whether square or round, these flaky knishes with delightful fillings bring back the taste of tradition. *Elzbieta Sekowska, Adobe stock.*

Two iconic Brooklyn images converge: the Brooklyn Bridge connecting Manhattan and Brooklyn and an authentic New York hot dog (forgive the ketchup). *Bernadett, Adobe Stock.*

Nathan's Fourth of July Hot Dog Eating Contest is more than one hundred years old—now that's a lot of hot dogs! *Wikimedia Commons.*

This is how New York's Eleven Madison Park, named the world's best restaurant in 2017, made its upscale version of the egg cream. *City Foodsters, Wikimedia Commons.*

These 1978 Dr. Brown's soda bottles show the full range of New York scenes depicted on their labels. *Herb Lubalin Syudy Center, Flickr.*

Above: Are they still black and whites when they represent every color of the rainbow? You bet! School colors, holidays, baby namings and brises—this cookie does it all. *Author's image.*

Left: Part of the twisted sisters duo, a slice of chocolate babka is simply heavenly. *Author's image.*

When the cheesecake is just right, it can stand alone (okay, a few berries couldn't hurt). *Alan Rosen, Junior's.*

An impressive display of halvah with different fillings and toppings. *Finn Stock, Adobe Stock.*

ROUNDING OUT THE MEAL

THE SIDEKICKS

*J*ust as the appetizing store experience was more than just smoked salmon, the same was true for the deli. While the meats were certainly the stars of the show, their sidekicks, such as that steaming bowl of soup to start the meal or the crunchy pickle that added an acidic bite, were just as integral. Every good deli had this supporting cast of characters, and businesses developed to meet the demand for products such as rye bread and tangy brown mustard. Here are some of the iconic foods that came to play. They elevate the sandwich, round out the meal and create the authentic deli experience.

THE OG OF JEWISH FOOD

Introducing a food that really needs to no introduction, as it's the dish most readily associated with eastern European Ashkenazi culture. This bowl defines many a deli experience, as you come in for the sandwich, but you come back for the soup—this liquid gold broth with bits of carrots and celery, a sweetness from onion, a luxuriousness from collagen-rich chicken bones and a bonus of dumplings that either float to the top or sink to the bottom. We're talking about matzo ball soup, which is iconic, period. What makes matzo ball soup emblematic of New York, you might ask? Every New York deli boasts about its version, every diner has it on its menu and even many upscale New York restaurants feature it prominently. Matzo ball soup is the ladleful that defines why New Yorkers raise a soup spoon. It is iconic to the Jewish culture and, by association, New York. So much so that it became the topic of many a Borscht Belt comedian, in-jokes that have been passed down from generation to generation like a well-worn Maxwell House Haggadah. Here's the most famous to make the rounds:

It's lunchtime and 70-year-old Moshe walks into Minky's Diner for his daily bowl of matzo ball soup. As usual, Moshe sits down at his table and smiles at Steve, his regular waiter. Almost immediately, a bowl of soup is placed in front of Moshe. But this time, as Steve is walking away, Moshe quickly calls him back to his table. "Please taste this soup," Moshe says to Steve. "Why?" asks Steve. "What's the matter with the soup? It's the same soup as you always have." "Please taste the soup," Moshe says again to Steve. "But there's nothing wrong with your soup. It's been made the same way we always make it," says Steve. "For the third time, Steve, I ask you to please taste the soup," says Moshe. "All right then…if you insist," says Steve, looking around the table. "But where's the spoon?" "Ah hah!" shouts Moshe with a big smile on his face.

Chicken soup came by the name "Jewish penicillin" naturally, as the soothing broth can make a sore throat feel better and the goodness in the ingredients are certainly nourishing and comforting. Maimonides, in the twelfth century, would recommend chicken soup for the weak and sick. It was a Sephardic tradition to feed it to women after childbirth and became an ingrained part of the Sephardic and Mizrahi tradition long before Ashkenazi Jews ever poached their first bird. By the fifteenth century, chicken soup had become a popular first course for Shabbat dinner. Therefore, it stands to reason when these same Jews immigrated to New York, they brought this tradition with them. Every Jewish deli in New York began featuring its version of chicken soup, and most served it with *kneidlach*, aka matzo balls. Matzo balls derived from German dumplings called *knodels*.

In eastern Europe, frugal cooks would use the matzo crumbs that were left over from Passover matzo to form their version of a dumpling. Some, as Esther Levy wrote in 1871, would simply soak whole pieces of matzo and use those as the basis for the dumplings. Those techniques remained the same when they immigrated to America. Supply follows demand, as indicated by food historian Andrew Smith. He noted that as early as 1859, "nine Jewish bakeries in New York used 2200 barrels of flour making matzah." Those sheets graced Passover tables and were used in the preparation of

Matzo ball soup, aka Jewish penicillin. *wEnDy, Flickr.*

matzo balls. Demand for matzo increased; that's when Streit's matzo, called by some as the "Jewish Plymouth Rock," was founded. It was established on the Lower East Side in 1916 by Austrian immigrant Aron Streit and his business associate Rabbi Moshe Weinberger. The Tenement Museum reports that Streit and Weinberger made each piece of matzo by hand in their Pitt Street facility. With the demand for their product increasing, in 1925 Streit's moved to a larger facility on Rivington, eventually occupying what was three tenement buildings and producing sixteen thousand pounds of matzo a day. You can be pretty sure that it was Streit's that supplied the delis that made the city's best matzo balls. The first use of the actual term *matzo ball* was in 1902, in *Mrs. Rorer's Cookbook* in a section devoted to Jewish recipes. It seemed to be a fitting name and stuck around. You might wonder if outside New York some unsophisticated diners are curious as to what other parts of the matzo are edible, other than the balls! New York matzo balls are rarely dainty, sometimes equaling the size of an orange, lean toward being floaters and are usually served in a bowl too small to hold the contents. That most likely explains the Yiddish joke that a *schlemiel* is someone who spills his chicken soup, while the *schlimazel* is the one he spills it on. The next time you seek out an authentic deli experience, be sure to start with the soup synonymous with New York—nope, not Manhattan clam chowder, but a steaming bowl of matzo ball soup.

What Am I, Chopped Liver?

A posh pot of chopped liver spread on crispy crostini. *Влаппена Азима, Flickr.*

That commonly used aphorism developed because of the deli experience. Chopped liver was never the central player in the deli case; it was often ignored, so the phrase refers to someone who is overlooked. Few if any people ever simply order a chopped liver sandwich, but many order one of the deli's great combos such as tongue and chopped liver. It was usually the sidekick, not the star. But good chopped liver can change the taste and texture of the sandwich. Consider the fact that kosher deli sandwiches didn't have the luxury of adding cheese and generally never added lettuce and tomato. So, chopped liver became the crowning glory of many a sandwich. It had a humble start. The livers, much like tongue, are offal and often discarded. In eastern Europe, where those who could not afford a quality cut of kosher meat needed cheap options, livers filled that void. At the start, it was goose liver that was transformed into a delicious delicacy. Much like foie gras, the goose would be fattened so the livers would be plump and rich. They were ground and mixed with *schmaltz* (rendered chicken fat) and served chilled. The French call it pâté, and the Jewish deli calls it a side dish.

Hold the Mayo

You can judge a classic deli by the tablescape, with clear plastic tumblers, paper napkins and always a small jar with a tiny spoon peeking out. Inside the jar is the mustard that is to be slathered generously on your sandwich; for deli goers, it is the king of condiments. Rabbi Solomon ben Isaac interpreted a passage from Genesis where Abraham serves mustard with tongue to the three angels that announced the birth of Jacob, so it's almost a commandment to do the same. One of America's original spicy mustards was created by Charles Gulden in 1862 in a shop on Elizabeth Street in New York. It's the dark grainy mustard that is the favorite of deli goers and is integral to the deli sandwich. Guldens was not the only spicy mustardteer (yes, I made that word up). Gold's, better known for its nose-clearing horseradish, marketed its version of deli mustard created in the 1930s from its operation in Brooklyn. Horseradish, one of Gold's original products, is often added to deli-style mustard to create that zing we associate with the condiment.

Ruth Glazer, in her 1946 article "The Jewish Delicatessen," reminisced about the deli that her dad opened on Long Island. She recalled that the job of creating what was called "poke" "toot" or "toddle" was given to the shop owner's kids. It comprised a small piece of wax paper twisted into a cone, crimped at the bottom and filled with mustard. "As soon as the youngsters of the family are old enough to hold two 'toots' of mustard in one hand and a ladle of mustard in the other, they are pressed into service." This conveyance of mustard was an iconic image for many a deli goer. What cream cheese is to the bagel and lox, mustard is to pastrami and rye. Mustard is the condiment that nine out of ten diners would say you must spread on your sandwich. The tenth diner, who says mayo, would be quickly ushered out of the deli and never allowed back. They say that anytime a deli customer asks for mayo on their sandwich, a Jew dies! Mayo, however, did come to fame during this same time, introduced to New York by German immigrant Richard Hellman. The story goes that Richard's wife, Margaret, the daughter of delicatessen owners, created this mixture of egg yolks and oil and began serving it to their patrons at a deli they established in 1920 on the UWS. According to the Hellman company, there were two versions, and Hellman put a blue ribbon on the one both he and his customers preferred. That image is still used today on its eponymous glass bottles of mayo.

With the advent of mayo, a Dutch dish called *koosla* (*kool*, which translates to mean cabbage, and *sla*, for salad) was transformed into the ubiquitous sidekick we know as coleslaw. The Dutch settlers grew cabbage near the Hudson River and mixed it with vinegar and spices. Once mayo became available in the early 1900s, it was introduced to the cabbage slaw and created a deli legend. Whether it is enjoyed as a sandwich topper or side dish, there wasn't a Jewish deli that didn't have it on hand. Here's a quick refresher: Do not ask for mayo in an authentic New York deli. Russian dressing (mayo mixed with ketchup) and mayo-laced coleslaw sure, but straight mayo never.

RYE DO YOU ASK?

For many a sandwich connoisseur, the bread is as crucial to the perfect sandwich as the meat. As Glazer noted:

> *It must here be understood that whereas your ordinary three-decker American sandwich of toasted white bread is considered a frivolity for leisured ladies at Schrafft's, there is nothing more serious (or deadly) than a three-decker sandwich of three slices of good rye bread. Its sheer weight makes superfluous the delicate toothpick. The delicatessen threedecker [sic] is served, meaningfully, with knife and fork, Compare, too, the contents. While the toasted sandwich can rely heavily on vegetable matter like lettuce and tomato to expand it to a respectable height, the delicatessen three-decker, by custom, is all meat.*

For more than a century, that bread of choice has been rye. Before the bagel gained a cult following, rye bread was king. The bread had to stand up to the mounds of meat, which at times could topple one pound. To feed this passion, Henry S. Levy founded Levy's Rye Bread in 1888 and situated it

One of Levy's groundbreaking ads. You don't have to be Jewish to love Levy's real Jewish rye, 1965. *Howard Zieff, photographer, Library of Congress.*

on Moore Street in Brooklyn. The company had an ingrained tradition of baking rye, pumpernickel and a long-gone favorite, cornbread, whose recipes they brought with them when they emigrated from Russia. The company was known for its provocative ad campaign that featured people of every background, race and ethnicity. The slogan that accompanied the posters plastered throughout New York in the 1960s was, "You don't have to be Jewish to love Levy's real Jewish rye." It was not only a successful campaign but a groundbreaking one. The big question you'll be asked when ordering a sandwich on rye is always, "Seeded or plain?" It's not a trick question, as there's no right or wrong. Some prefer the pungent caraway seeds classic in seeded rye, while others prefer not to use dental floss in public.

If you were looking for an artisanal version of classic bread, look no further than Orwasher's, who has been baking and breaking bread with its Yorkville neighbors since 1916. Abraham Orwasher, an immigrant from Hungary, was not a baker by trade, according to an interview given by his son Louis in 1994 with Anne Hecht for the Oral History of the American Jewish Committee. Louis described his father, who needed to support seven children, as a very dedicated and hard worker at the bakery then owned by Isadore Gelber. When Abe bought the bakery from Gelber, he also bought what Louis called "the original formulas," which they are still making today in the same ovens from 1916. Louis aptly described the Upper East Side neighborhood of the early to mid-1900s, where the store originated:

> *From 68th to 71st was mostly Czech. 71st to 75th was a little mixture of Czech and Italian. 75th to 79th was Italian and then starting to blend with Hungarian, and the Hungarian people went up as far as around 82nd, 83rd, and then you blended in with the German people. So you had the different bakeries baking the native product of the people in the area…you had a bakery every three blocks.*

It's rumored that Louis actually created pumpernickel raisin bread, a version that is still prominent in the store today. Orwasher's continues to produce hearth-baked bread and other bakery delights for area residents on the UES and UWS. It supplies many of New York's restaurants with freshly baked bread to the tune of ten thousand loaves per day.

I'm Also a Big Dill

The star of any pickling barrel would have to be the namesake of the process, the pickle. According to Gil Marks, the word derived from a northern German word meaning "salt and brine." That certainly makes sense, as those are two major players in the pickling process. Pickles serve a real purpose as palate cleansers, preventing the pungent meats from dulling the taste buds. Once Ashkenazi Jews discovered the goodness of a pickled cucumber, they made it a mainstay in their diet. Claudia Roden called pickles "so representative of Jewish food that they have come to symbolize it." However, it was most likely the Dutch who began pickling cucumbers in New York as far back as the seventeenth century. According to Untappedcities.com, they would grow the cucumbers in Brooklyn and sell the pickles in local markets. At the turn of the century, pickles could be bought for a penny, making them a fast, easy street food and a favorite of Jewish immigrants. The smells of the Lower East Side were a rare perfume of smoked meats, pickled fish and salty brine from the barrels of pickles sold by pushcart vendors on Essex Street. The stretch was dubbed "Pickle Alley," as it's estimated that eighty pickle vendors dotted the street.

One of those pickle sellers was Izzy Guss, a Russian immigrant who established one of the first pickle stands on the Lower East Side. By 1920, he had a storefront on Hester, where it remained until the 2000s. Most recently, Guss' has been resurrected and ships its true New York pickles across the country. When I spoke to Andrew Leibowitz of Guss', I asked why he thinks pickles are so iconic to New York. He quickly answered, "Because everyone loves pickles." Who can argue with that logic? In talking with Alan Kaufman—a Guss' alumni, native "Queenser," pickle expert and current owner of the Pickle Guys—you realize that there's more to the pickle than meets the eye. The Pickle Guys currently sells forty-five varieties of pickled foods, which it brines just steps away from where Guss' got its start. After more than forty years in the business, Alan has pickle juice running in his veins, as well as some particularly good pickle advice. "I'm

Goes to show that the Pickle Guys can pickle anything. The barrels go on the length of the store. *Author's image.*

a little bit of a snob," he admitted, "I match pickles with what I'm eating. Pastrami or tuna salad calls for a sour pickle; with its strong flavor, it cuts through the salt. Burgers get a half sour, so the beefy taste comes through. And on a pleasant day, eat a new pickle for its clean, refreshing taste." What's the most underrated pickle he sells? He pointed to the horseradish pickle, which he says is great in a bloody Mary.

In visiting the Pickle Guys, I found some unexpected foods swimming in their large red barrels, such as pickled baby corn and okra, as well as many types of pickled cucumbers and tomatoes. You can choose not only new, half-sour and sour pickles, but a three-quarter-sour pickle, something rarely found anyplace else. If you go, be sure to ask for samples of some of the more exotic foods, like pickled string beans or turnips.

Not just pushcart vendors or LES institutions sold pickles to meet the demand. In 1955, Ba-Tampte began turning out its classic New York pickles in a plant based in Brooklyn, where they are still produced today. Kaufman recalled his mother buying one jar of Ba-Tampte pickled tomatoes and wondering where they went after just a day. He wisely advised her to start buying two to satisfy his pickle habit. Ba-Tampte has carried on the family tradition that began when the owners' grandfather manned a pushcart on the LES. Even if you're not within whiffing distance of a pickle seller, don't sour on the subject. Today, you can find many varieties of Jewish deli–style pickles in your local market. Sifting through the varieties at your grocer can be jarring, but keep looking—they are worth the effort and you'll relish the experience!

Not to be overlooked for its role as part of the deli and hot dog experience is pickled cabbage, better known as sauerkraut. The process of pickling cabbage dates back to ancient China, where it's reported that cabbage was fermented during the construction of the Great Wall. The word *sauerkraut* can be traced to the German for sour cabbage, and it was most likely German immigrants who brought it to America. Sauerkraut is integral to making the perfect Reuben or adding an acidic bite to your hot dog.

~~~

21st-Century Baller

This recipe finds the balance between floaters and sinkers and is so easy to make.

3 large eggs
3 tablespoons chicken fat at room temperature (you can sub a neutral oil, but chicken fat adds so much flavor)
1 teaspoon kosher salt
½ teaspoon garlic powder
¼ teaspoon black pepper
1 tablespoon seltzer water
1 cup plus 2 tablespoons matzo meal
3 tablespoons Osem consommé base

A simmering pot of knodels, aka kneidlach, aka matzo balls. *Phelsuma Laticauda, Flickr.*

Whisk the first five ingredients together. Add the seltzer water and then gently stir in the matzo meal and mix until it resembles thick cookie dough.

Place the bowl in the fridge while you bring a large pot of about 4 quarts of water to boil, with the Osem dry soup base. This is a great way to flavor the matzo balls with a chicken soup taste while not consuming your freshly brewed batch of soup.

When the water is boiling, wet your hands with water or a dab of oil and begin rolling the matzo balls, about the size of a walnut. Do not over roll; simply smush the mixture to form the balls and drop into the water. Reduce the heat to a strong simmer, cover and cook 30 to 40 minutes.

Cut into one matzo ball to be sure it is no longer doughy. If it is cooked through, remove with a slotted spoon and set aside until ready to use. If it appears doughy, cook an additional 5 to 10 minutes. To serve, let them cook in the actual soup for at least 15 minutes.

To freeze, let them cool and then place on a parchment-lined tray and freeze. Once frozen, place them in an airtight bag. To thaw, simply drop them in your soup and allow them to cook through.

SECOND TO NONE

DAIRY, DYNAMIC AND DISGUISED

*N*ot everyone was on team delicatessen. Some preferred a restaurant experience focused on non-meat offerings, especially for those who kept kosher. For those observant Jews, the kosher-style deli where meat and dairy were mixing was not an option. To get their cheese blintz fix outside the home, they needed to find a dairy-only restaurant, an establishment that flourished in New York in the early to mid-1900s. There were also those who wanted a less proletarian option, and for them the deli might have been a bit déclassé. They were seeking out a more dynamic American experience, with glitz and glamour and a bit of naughty. And a third group were looking for an entirely different dining option altogether, one that didn't just think outside the box—it completely disassembled it. It took their assimilation to the brink through disguised food while establishing a custom that began in New York and stands today. These restaurant choices didn't run a distant second to the deli—they were unique New York food options in their own right and made a lasting imprint.

Dairy Queens

If the prototypical deli was built on pastrami, corned beef and tongue, then its counterpart, the dairy restaurant, had a foundation layered with latkes, blintzes and gefilte fish. This preference for meatless menus, as noted by

Ziegelman, conveniently coincided with a tremendous increase in the price of kosher meat that took place in 1902. At that time, East Side housewives organized citywide boycotts and protested with picketers stationed in front of neighborhood butcher shops. So intense was the fight that those who dared cross the picket line and purchase from these shops found their groceries doused with kerosene. The rage ensued for another decade, as New York gave rise to the popularity of dairy restaurants. There the diner could get comforting favorites like kugel and borscht. Ben Katchor's *The Dairy Restaurant* listed some famous patrons of this vegetarian approach to dining. That included Leon Trotsky, who briefly lived in Upper Manhattan before returning to Russia after the 1917 revolution. He had an affinity for kosher dairy restaurants and frequented the Triangle Dairy in the East Bronx. It was said that the avowed Marxist did not tip, as he felt it was an indignity to the waiter. In turn, "the waiters retaliated with poor service, accidental spillings [*sic*] of hot soup and insults."

The big three of the dairy restaurants were the latke, blintz and gefilte fish. The latke has long been a standard at Chanukah and the single best excuse for eating fried foods—who can argue with a miracle? But at a New York City dairy deli, you could find it year-round. Latkes, aka potato pancakes, became very popular in eastern Europe during the mid-1800s, when potatoes were cheap and plentiful. Restaurants in New York would churn out fresh latkes in all sizes, some as big as your plate, with mountains of sour cream or fresh apple sauce. They became such a symbol of New York food culture that, for years, the highly regarded James Beard Foundation would run an annual Hanukkah Latke Lover's Cook-Off that garnered tremendous media attention.

The blintz was another favorite. This cousin to the Russian blini or French crêpe would feature a host of fillings from potato or cheese to jammy fruits, all topped with a dollop of sour cream. They were the Jewish dairy restaurant's answer to the American pancake, which was topped with syrupy preserves or folded with breakfast-style fillings. Blintzes got their start, according to Gil Marks, in the fourteenth century when Turks conquered the Balkans and were introduced to a thin wheat pancake, filled and rolled. It evolved as it traveled east to the area of Ukraine, where its name became *blintze*, before settling in New York. Both latkes and blintzes can be found in almost every grocery store's frozen food section, but they are a far cry from the fresh-made ones served in the Jewish dairy restaurant.

Another popular offering, which is available on almost every supermarket shelf, is gefilte fish. Claudia Roden reminded us that gefilte fish, when

A look into Ratner's menu. *NYPL, Digital Collection, Rare Book Division.*

first prepared in medieval times, featured chopped freshwater fish, stuffed into the skin of pike or carp. It should be no surprise, then, that *gefilte* translates from the Yiddish to mean stuffed. It became a staple of Sabbath meals, and eventually that labor-intensive process was refined to forming patties, or, as the French would say, *quenelles*. That is the form Ashkenazi immigrants brought with them to New York. It became a popular option at the dairy restaurant. Gefilte fish begged for pungent horseradish, which encouraged Gold's to begin producing its product in 1932, made in a Brooklyn apartment. New York is still the place where you can find house-made gefilte fish not just during the holidays but every day.

Unlike these top three sellers, there's one dish that no one continues to seek out but was a favorite at the dairy restaurant. It was made from bits of toast soaked in a bowl of hot milk. Known as "milk toast" on the menu, the dish's name morphed into milquetoast an insult for a bland and timid man.

The dairy restaurants were concentrated below Houston, an area we now call Soho and East of the Bowery. Katchor quoted a 1919 *New York Tribune* article describing the typical dairy restaurant, saying that they all bore "a striking sameness, with their stained woodwork, marble-topped tables crowned with little baskets of rolls." The first dairy restaurant was owned by Jacob Kampus, who was quite the promoter. An 1890 ad in the *Worker's Newspaper* read, "Where are you going? To Jacob Kampus. For What? To find their good blintzes, kreplach or mamaliga….When you want to convince yourself it's good and tasty come to the world-famous Romanian blintz-maker." Most dairy-only restaurants are gone now; however, one of the first, and still standing, is B&H, a kosher dairy restaurant that opened on 2nd Avenue in 1938. Despite seeing the neighborhood change and the customer base dwindle, it holds fast to its original menu. A sign of the times is the current ownership, which comprises a Polish Christian woman, a Muslim and a Mexican man, which sounds like the basis for a politically incorrect joke. However, this team maintains the standards and menu that made B&H a destination. When asked why they continue the kosher tradition, Ola, one of the owners, answered, "The original owners started this restaurant kosher, so now we stay kosher." The pandemic took a toll on the restaurant, and a GoFundMe drive kept the business afloat. That's a testament to what they mean to the community, and their tenacity indicates what the community means to them.

Unfortunately, two known greats were not able to survive the changing times, that being Ratner's and Rapoport's. Jacob Harmatz founded Ratner's in 1905, along with his brother-in-law Alex Ratner. They found a permanent home in 1928 on Delancey, where at the height of its popularity, it could serve up to 1,200 people per day. A well-known secret was a speakeasy that operated in the back room of the restaurant. Jewish mobsters such as Meyer Lansky and Bugsy Siegel would gather along with Italian gangster Lucky Luciano. In a posting on Portable NYC, the writer asked us to consider that "while eating baked whitefish in the back room of Ratner's Meyer Lansky…was quietly masterminding his criminal enterprise." This was truly an "only in New York" possibility. In 2002, the *New York Times* reported the restaurant closing with a woeful headline: "The other latke finally dropped on Delancey Street Yesterday." Citing the migration of Jewish New Yorkers to points north, the owners reluctantly decided to close.

Harry Rapoport founded their dairy restaurant in 1923, having saved enough money working as a waiter after he arrived in New York. Speaking to his grandson Burt, who today is a successful restaurateur, was like going back in time. He described dinners at home being dinner at the restaurant, as they lived above the store. Sometimes up to twelve family members would dine together and order off the menu just as the customers would. Burt remembers his favorite meal being their bagel with cream cheese, Nova and sturgeon. His grandfather would kiddingly yell, "You've ordered the most expensive thing on the menu!" and then tell the waiter, "Bring him potato soup!" Despite sounding stingy with his grandson, Harry's charity was legendary. During the Depression, if a patron bought a cup of coffee for a nickel, they could sit and eat all the rolls they desired from the baskets placed on the tables. Sadly, as the neighborhood lost many of their Jewish residents in the 1970s, the restaurant closed. It seems ironic that with the advent of vegetarianism, the dairy restaurant of the early 1900s might be a hot spot today.

Dynamic Dining

In the world of iconic dining institutions, not everyone fell into the deli or dairy category. There were many restaurants that blurred the lines, offering more upscale fare in less predictable spaces. They attracted customers who were stepping out of their comfort zone and into the ideal of an American one. They were often star studded, usually non-kosher and always making headlines. It would be remiss not to give a nod to a few that helped create a mystique around Jewish food, making it glamorous, upscale and crave worthy. They did this by appealing to a celebrity base, mostly Jewish intellectuals, artists, musicians and actors—many of whom flourished on stage in the Yiddish theater along 2nd Avenue. The first that comes to mind is Café Royale, lovingly known as the "Jewish Delmonico's" or the "Yiddish Sardi's." Everyone from Walter Matthau to Isaac Bashevis Singer would hold court there while enjoying mounds of Hungarian goulash. Author Leo Rosten once said of the restaurant, "To be seen there was a social duty, a mark of distinction and an investment in prestige."

Another restaurant representative of the times was Reuben's, whose motto was "From a Sandwich to a National Institution." Born in Germany, owner Arnold Reuben (you might remember him from a previous chapter as the man who did not invent the Reuben sandwich) immigrated to America around 1886 and worked various jobs before opening his first restaurant in 1908. He was the ultimate restaurateur and showman and owned and operated several restaurants in addition to his crowning glory, Reuben's. It's rumored that gangster Arnold Rothstein plotted to fix the 1919 Baseball World Series at one of Reuben's outposts. In 1922, Reuben was suspected of breaking Prohibition law, as an article in the *New York Times* revealed. He claimed to be innocent, saying that the flasks had been "planted." After a number of iterations and moves, his namesake restaurant had a formal opening in 1935 on East 58th Street with Mayor La Guardia in attendance. The restaurant deviated from the typical format, as it was posh, with a doorman greeting you at the front and a glitzy, gilded interior. His lengthy menu featured the usual suspects, as well as pronounced *treyf* (non-kosher food) such as pig's knuckles and littleneck clams. But what Reuben's was most known for were the Reuben Specials, new and inventive sandwich combinations, many named for celebrities like the Frank Sinatra, with cream cheese, Bar-le-Duc (jelly), tongue and sweet pickle on whole wheat bread, or the Judy Garland, mixing Nova and Swiss cheese. In 1938, Arnold gave an interview to American Life Histories:

Above: Reuben's menu reflected the assimilated tastes of New Yorkers and the celebrities who flocked there. *NYPL, Digital Collection, Rare Book Division.*

Opposite: Small pitchers of schmaltz placed on restaurant tables such as Sammy's Romanian. *Mimi Zeiger, Flickr.*

Manuscripts from the Federal Writer's Project 1936–1940, and explained the evolution of a Reuben Special:

> I'll tell you about how I got the sandwich idea…one day a dame walks in, one of the theatrical dames…she asks me for something to eat. Her name was Anna Selos.… I'm clowning for the dame. Well, what do I do? I take a holy bread…I cut it right through on the bias. Then I take some roast beef, I don't remember exactly what. But, anyway, I figure I'll put anything on it. So I take some meat and cheese and I slap it on, and I put on some spice and stuff and I make her up a sandwich; it was a foot high. Well the dame just eats it, that's all.…When she gets through, she says, "Mr. Reuben, that the best sandwich I ever tasted in my life." Well, the idea comes to me in a flash.… Well, boys, in a flash, I get the idea.…I'll call it a Reuben Special.

Reuben didn't as much break the mold as obliterate it. He earned a loyal following, most likely because of rather than despite his larger-than-life appeal to a less homogenized clientele.

Another type of Jewish restaurant that influenced the way New Yorkers ate in the 1900s was the Romanian steakhouse. The best known was Moskowitz & Lupowitz, which sounds more like a law firm than a restaurant. Opened in 1909 by Romanian immigrants, it was the hangout of celebrities, both Jewish and not, as Bing Crosby was a regular along with Milton Berle and Sid Caesar. The usual fare was featured along with Romanian steak, a specialty made famous in New York Jewish steakhouses. When these establishments closed, a unique New York restaurant took their place. Sammy's Roumanian

was trying to be a spot for younger guests to enjoy LES nightlife, older ones to immerse themselves in nostalgia and everyone to break the rules. Beloved by New Yorkers and crowded with tourists, every night at Sammy's was, as *Food and Wine Magazine* declared, like being at a bar mitzvah! That is, if the bar mitzvah boy favored loud disco music (yes, they had a disco ball), a cramped basement to dine in and syrup jars filled with schmaltz. I recall (or barely recall, as the vodka that night flowed like water) a night at Sammy's where we devoured *kreplach* (stuffed dumpling) and Romanian steak amid a rousing atmosphere. While none of these places continues to exist, they served a purpose in glorifying traditional and not-so-traditional Jewish foods to a hungry city. They elevated what some considered to be humble offerings, created dynamic eating adventures and shared them with a clientele that would spread the word.

Disguised Delicacies

If a food can be iconic, and the restaurants like those we just explored can achieve the same status, can we extend our definition to an established food custom that dances on the edge of inclusion? Can we consider a tradition that began in New York and has spread across the country under this broad umbrella? If we don't, it would be like trying to prepare lo mein without the noodles—something would be missing. So, let's take a moment to trace the origin and the lasting impact of a restaurant tradition that can be traced to New York in the early 1900s. There's an old joke that Arthur Schwartz shared: "If according to the Jewish calendar the year is 5764, and according to the Chinese calendar the year is 5724, what did Jews eat for forty years?" Like all humor, there's tremendous truth in the joke, and it all started in New York. The crowded Lower East Side, teeming with Jewish immigrants, was steps from Chinatown, where Asian Americans settled. Both groups shared a feeling of being outsiders, as they formed the two largest non-Christian populations at the time. Aside from this sociological connection, they shared similarities that extended into their cuisines. Neither mixed dairy and meat, and Chinese food, much like eastern European, leaned heavily on chicken, vegetables, onions, broth and the combination of sweet and sour. Additionally, most other ethnic restaurants were closed on Sunday nights, but the Chinese restaurants remained opened and welcomed their Jewish neighbors.

Perhaps the biggest draw was that Chinese food gave Jewish diners the chance to make a foray into non-kosher food without tremendous guilt. Like dipping a toe in a cold lake before taking the plunge, the less observant Jewish diner could enjoy a wonton stuffed with…well, who knew what? The pork was minced and the spareribs coated—the non-kosher food was wearing a disguise. They could look at a wonton as if it were a kreplach and allow the soup to wash down the dumplings as well as the guilt. Sociologist Gaye Tuchman called this "plausible deniability" and termed Chinese food "safe *treyf.*"

Not everyone was happy about this trend. Hasia Diner noted that *Der Tog*, a New York daily Yiddish paper, ran an article entitled "*Di Milkhome tsvishn*

Jewish kreplach or Chinese wontons—plausible deniability. *Liz Rueven, @kosherlikeme.*

Tshap-sui un Gefilte Fish," which means "The War between Chop Suey and Gefilte Fish." The article, although tongue-in-cheek, questioned Jews who were moving away from the old-world traditions. An outgrowth of this weekly Sunday night ritual became a yearly one, and it transformed how generations of Jewish people spend Christmas. Rabbi Joshua Plaut, author of *A Kosher Christmas*, placed the tradition squarely on the Lower East Side as far back as 1899. According to Plaut, eating Chinese food on Christmas morphed into a way for Jewish diners to feel like they had a secular tradition to mark the holiday. No tree or mistletoe—just a steaming bowl of wonton soup. They were no longer left out of Christmas. They simply redefined it with their own tradition. Just remember, the next time you enjoy Christmas with General Tsao, you have the Jewish immigrants of the Lower East Side to thank.

Even though Jewish diners filled the seats at neighborhood Chinese restaurants, Solomon Bernstein took the relationship to the next level and introduced kosher Chinese food to New York. In 1959, he opened the famous Bernstein's on Essex, but many called it Schmulka Bernstein's in honor of Solomon's father. Waiters wore kitschy tasseled caps (in lieu of yarmulkes), and beef, veal and chicken livers substituted for pork, As Bernstein said of their restaurant, *"Kashrut* was king and quality reigns." Observant Jewish diners could enjoy kosher versions of their Cantonese favorites. The

Times once quoted the restaurant manager, David Gurfein, as saying that he couldn't teach kosher cooks to cook Chinese food, so instead, he hired Chinese cooks from the Catskills who knew a thing or two about kosher cooking. The restaurant closed in the late 1900s, but its influence on the way Jewish New Yorkers ate was indelible. Kosher Chinese restaurants now abound in New York, as do hybrids that are putting their own spin on the mashup of cuisines. So, if your wonton speaks Yiddish, you now know why.

Florence Tabrys' Blintzes

(Reprinted by permission from Recipes Remembered: A Celebration of Survival, *June Hersh, Ruder Finn Press, May 2011)*

Blintzes were the darlings of the dairy restaurant, and for good reason. They have a pillowy, comforting quality as a delicious breakfast, decadent brunch or light lunch offering. Top them with sour cream or fresh fruit and celebrate the Ashkenazi interpretation of a French crêpe.

Yields 10 blintzes.

For the Batter:

6 large eggs
½ cup warm water
½ cup whole milk
1 cup all-purpose flour

For the Filling:

4-ounces cream cheese, room temperature
1 cup farmer's cheese
1 teaspoon melted butter
¾ teaspoon ground cinnamon
1 egg, beaten

Butter for frying
1 tray lined with paper towels

A plate of blintzes waiting to be filled or enjoyed as is. Fancy table setting optional. *Elina Fairytale, Pexils.com.*

Prepare the batter by whisking together all the ingredients. The batter should be thinner than traditional pancake batter. Refrigerate while you prepare the filling. For the filling, combine all the ingredients and blend until smooth.

Heat a nub of butter in an 8-inch nonstick skillet. Ladle about ¼ cup batter into the center of the pan and quickly swirl to evenly distribute batter. Fry for 1 minute and then flip. Cook for 30 seconds on the second side and remove to the waiting paper towel. Cover with a second paper towel to prevent the pancake from drying out. Add more butter and follow the process until you have used all the batter.

When cool to the touch, begin filling the blintzes. Plop a large tablespoon of filling right in the middle of the blintze. Bring the two ends to the middle and then fold the two sides to the middle, creating an oblong package. Don't worry if they are irregularly shaped—that's how people know it's homemade. When all blintzes are wrapped, they are ready to fry. Heat several nubs of butter in the skillet and fry for several minutes on each side seam side down first, until golden brown.

Enjoy with a dollop of sour cream lightly sweetened with cinnamon and sugar, dust with confectioner's sugar, grate a little orange zest or top with fresh fruit. They are the perfect canvas for any topping.

THE BIG HISTORY OF A SMALL NOSH

KNISH AND TELL

*D*id you hear the one about the dinner party at the Jones' house, where they set the table for six people, until the host was informed that one of her guests was bringing twelve knishes? Unfamiliar with Jewish food, she quickly reset her table for eighteen! That could very well be a true story for the uninitiated who live outside New York and have never had the singular pleasure of digging into a fresh-baked knish. Whether you call it bite-sized comfort food or New York's favorite nosh, you need to try one in the city that made them famous to understand how and why they have become such a popular food and withstood the test of time.

Let's start with the basics: what exactly is a knish? It's like the empanada, as it is dough that is stuffed. It's reminiscent of a pierogi, as potato and onion are the most popular filling. But it is truly a food of its own making. Joanna O'Leary in writing about *The History of the Humble Knish in America*, admitted that "the exact composition of this dish is…nebulous…a softball-size lump of dough, that may be baked or deep-fried…packed with mashed potatoes or kasha…however, there are no rules when it comes to stuffing." Gil Marks wrote that "the knish is an example of classic peasant food evolving into comfort food and even sophisticated fare." So, where did it evolve from and how did it get here?

The knish originated in the areas known as the Pale of Settlement (western regions of the former Russian empire), where it was called *knysz*. It might have found its way there when Jews were expelled from France in the fourteenth century. Perhaps no one on the planet is more an expert on the origin of the

You've arrived at Knyszyn. Hop off the train and enjoy a knish. *Henryk Borawski, Wikimedia Commons.*

knish than author Laura Silver, who in her book *Knish: In Search of Jewish Soul Food* explored every nook and cranny of this coveted dough pie. She traced its roots to a town in Poland aptly named Knyszyn. It stands to reason that if the town called itself Knishtown, it must have been where it was perfected. Silver wrote that monks in Ukraine "rode from one manor house to the next, trick or treat style, asking for offerings. Yes, knishes." There were mini knishes stuffed with cabbage, cheese and dill that became a Christian ritual food, as well as those made during Lent filled with sheep's milk cheese, herbs and mashed potato. But it is possible that the first verifiable mention came in the form of a poem, "Krakowiec Guild," from a town close to Lviv, present-day Ukraine. It's illustrative of how much a cross-cultural food the knish is:

> *They get so confused, they know not their own minds,*
> *One celebrates with a Jew, and at night with a Lutheran dines.*
> *The next day, it's knishes with the Orthodox priest-man,*
> *And so, each one knows not where he stands.*

As knishes adapted to kosher life in Poland and the surrounding areas, the fillings tended more toward vegetarian, and those are the versions that found their way to America. They became the darlings of pushcart vendors who had a compartment where the knishes were kept separate from hot dogs or pretzels. What started as a Jewish immigrant food quickly became a favorite among New Yorkers across cultural lines. Knishes are the ultimate street food—no condiments required (although mustard goes nicely), no bread or bun needed, no fork or knife and no etiquette in enjoying. It's the Swiss Army knife of foods.

The knish is a food enigma, as there are no real standards in preparation, but there are standard-bearers. The first would have to be New York's Yonah Schimmel, who brought it to its rightful place as an iconic New York food. Schimmel was a Romanian rabbi, and he sold his wife's round baked knishes from his pushcart in the late 1800s. Schimmel was so renowned that guidebooks would promote "nostalgic tours" of the neighborhood, as Suzanne Wasserman wrote in *Remembering the Lower East Side*. One of the musts was Yonah Schimmel. Visitors from as far as California would arrive in New York "bearing…the address of a recommended hotel and of Yoineh Shimmel's [*sic*] knish emporium." Wasserman continued to quote Nathan Ausubel, who then said that even New Yorkers from "the remote corners of the Bronx" come to Schimmel's. "They come with the hungry piety of pilgrims." The LES, especially Rivington and Stanton, became knish central. While the neighborhood changed and turned over during the twentieth century, time stood still for the first purveyor and the last man standing, Yonah Schimmel. Schimmel still turns out the beloved traditional knish from the store he established in 1910, faithful to the first they sold. My recent visit there was met by a group of tourists on a food tour of the LES. When I asked one what they thought a knish was, she took a good guess and said "wheat with potato." After she tried her very first, she gave it two thumbs up. Schimmel's has also changed with the neighborhood and the times in offering everything from jalapeño cheddar to chocolate cheese knishes. It's such a New York institution that even the sign of his eponymous store was immortalized by the painter Hedy Pagremanski and is a part of the Museum of the City of New York's permanent collection.

Like most other food development, knishes were not without controversy and rivalry. In a 1916 article in the *New York Times*, the knish made headlines: "Rivington St. Sees War." The fracas was centered on two knish sellers, Max Green and Morris London, who went dough to dough. Not only did they undercut each other on price, but they resorted to theatrical tricks like oompah bands and cabaret singers to attract customers. Eventually, the war ceased, and everyone lived in perfect knish harmony.

The window at Yonah Schimmel's century-old knishery; it wasn't Zagat rated back then. *Wikimedia Commons.*

In Brooklyn, another knish maker was making waves on Coney Island. In 1921, the Sephardi couple Elias and Bella Gabay went from being shoemakers to producing square knishes. Originally, the knishes were made in Bella's LES kitchen and then sold on a pushcart. They began selling their knishes to delis across the city and in 1928 moved to a true facility in Brooklyn, naming the company Gabila's. They were the innovators of an automated knish machine to meet the overwhelming demand for their product. Today, Gabila's is the world's largest knish producer, making more than 15 million per year, all based on Bella's original lightly seasoned mashed potato filling. The self-proclaimed "king of potato pies," the company has sold more than 1 billion knishes—take that McDonald's!

While we're in Brooklyn paying homage to the knish, it's worth noting Mrs. Stahl's, the beloved, although now defunct, knishery, which was located under the tracks at Brighton Beach. Mrs. Stahl, like so many others before her, prepared her recipe at home and sold them as a street vendor on the beach in the 1930s. Her store was a legend for more than fifty years before closing its doors. One last knishery also deserves mentioning for those who find themselves in Queens with a hankering for a knish. Knish Nosh has been a landmark there for seventy years and has become a mini chain turning out knishes. You can even grab one on the go in New York's farthest southern borough, Palm Beach County.

Perhaps no woman showed as much knish gumption as Gussie Schwebel (neé Sussman), who, unaware of the success of Yonah Schimmel just a few blocks away, thought that she had a novel idea to make knishes. She attracted a host of illustrious knish-eating customers to Houston Street, as Silver pointed out, including then New York City police chief Teddy Roosevelt and celebrities like Enrico Caruso and Marxist revolutionary Leon Trotsky. She once told the *New York Post* in 1941 that a line of Rolls-Royces would wrap around the block to sample her knishes, earning her the self-ascribed "Queen of Knishes." She felt it appropriate to reach out to another famous woman of the time, First Lady Eleanor Roosevelt. She wrote, "I wonder if I may not be able to be of service to my beloved land, by way of introducing the knish, which is very wholesome and not costly to produce into the diet of our armed forces." Now that's patriotism, chutzpah and entrepreneurship. After several exchanges, the first lady agreed, via telegram, to accept a delivery of knishes at her UES apartment at precisely 5:00 p.m. Tuesday, January 27, 1942. Unfortunately, the story did not have the ending Schwebel had hoped for. Roosevelt was perturbed by all the media attention and turned the delivery away.

Despite this personal disappointment for Schwebel, the knish continued its political legacy. The phenomenon known as "knish politics," a term discussed in an article in *The Forward*, explains a campaign connection to the knish. For politicians looking to show that they are regular people and additionally court the Jewish vote, they make an obligatory pilgrimage to Schimmel's to be photographed eating a knish. It's said that no politician can win an election without checking this box. Ironically, Jewish candidate for governor Robert Morgenthau failed to do so and lost his bid to a knish-eating Gentile, Nelson Rockefeller. Could it have been bad knish karma? If you're ambitious, here's a great recipe to try making Mrs. Stahl's original knishes. Breathe deeply when preparing and you might even smell the Brighton Beach salt air.

~~~

Mrs. Stahl's Knishes

The recipe here was adapted from one re-created by Fannie Stahl, one of Mrs. Stahl's granddaughters. It was then tweaked by Toby Engelberg and Sara Spatz. The finished recipe below has been excerpted from Knish: In Search of the Jewish Soul Food *by Laura Silver (Brandeis University Press/University Press of New England, 2014).*

For the Dough:

3¼ cups flour
1 tablespoon sugar
1 teaspoon salt
½ cup vegetable oil
1 cup lukewarm water

For the Filling:

6 pounds russet or new potatoes
1 cup oil
¼ cup salt, or to taste
1½ teaspoons pepper
8 cups raw onions, thinly sliced
Vegetable oil and flour as needed for assembling and baking

Turn on the oven on a low temperature until the dough is ready. Mix flour, sugar and salt. Add oil and water. Mix with a spoon until the dough pulls together or use a food processor or stand mixer (with a dough hook). Turn out the dough on board and knead it, incorporating all pieces. Knead until dough is one piece, smooth and glossy. Turn off the oven. Oil the dough and place it in oiled, covered bowl. Place in oven until you are ready to use it. Let the dough rest at least 2 hours; the dough should barely rise, if at all. Keeping the dough overnight in the refrigerator is fine. Bring it back to room temperature before use.

Scrub the potatoes and peel them, unless the new potatoes have very thin, unblemished skins. Boil potatoes for about 20 minutes until knife tender and then drain. Mash with a potato masher. Add oil, salt and pepper to taste. Mix. Stir in the onion.

Preheat oven to 450°F. Position one rack in lower third and one in upper third of oven. Roll out about half the dough on a lightly floured counter or tabletop. Roll with handle-less rod-style rolling pin out from the center until dough is thin enough to see through, about 1/16-inch thick.

Oil top edge of dough with a pastry brush. Place a 2-inch-diameter line of filling about 2 inches from the top edge of the dough. Pick up top edge and drape over filling. Brush oil on dough in a 2-inch strip on the bottom edge of the filling. Pick up the dough with filling and roll again onto the oiled dough, compressing the filled dough as you turn it. Repeat until the dough covers the filling three to four times, being sure always to brush oil on the dough first. Use a knife to separate the filled potato knish log from the remaining dough. Cut off edges of filled dough. Cut the filled roll into pieces about 6 inches long and coil each piece like a snail's shell. Tuck the remaining end into the bottom of the coil. Alternatively, place stuffed roll of dough onto ungreased cookie sheet and slash with a knife crosswise every 2 inches. Leave an inch of space between each roll or coil of dough.

Bake 20 to 25 minutes until the knish skin is browned and knishes are cooked through, starting knishes on lowest rack of the over and raising them to top rack after about 10 to 12 minutes. Let the knishes cool in pan. If you cooked the knishes in long rolls, cut them into individual pieces.

Knishes can be reheated in the oven or in a skillet on the stovetop.

WE'RE STUFFED

SAUSAGE

MAKING THE BEST WURST

What do Italian pepperoni, British bangers and frankfurters all have in common? If you say that they are the foods that a cardiologist's nightmares are made of, you would be right. But if you knew they were all forms of sausage, you would be correct as well. Any mixture that is ground and encased qualifies as sausage. So those hot dogs, salami and bologna we enjoy are all types of sausage. The most famous New York sausage is the hot dog. There is a reason that everyone has on their food bucket list a Coney Island frank or a hot dog at Yankee Stadium. They are embedded in our food culture and certainly rank as iconic New York food. Whether you call them franks (designates that they came from Frankfurter, Germany), wieners (those are from Vienna) or hot dogs, the most Americanized name, we can all agree that when they slide into a fresh bun, are tossed with baked beans or topped with a schmear of mustard, blanketed in sauerkraut and snap as you devour it in three large bites, it doesn't get any better than that.

When hot dogs burst onto the New York scene, they came with a very long lineage of sausage making in Europe. Tracing its roots could take us back thousands of years, when Judeans ate *naknik*, the Hebrew word for sausage. But it found true popularity when fifteenth-century Germans created bratwurst and its rhyming cousin knockwurst. Most sausage of those times was made with pork products and fillers, while Jewish sausages called *vurst* were made with kosher beef. As German Jews and non-Jews came to New York, they

Mayor Fiorello La Guardia created quite a crowd surge as he stopped by a hot dog stand in 1935. *NYPL, Digital Collection, Manuscript and Archives Division.*

brought the laborious tradition of sausage making with them. At the start, chopping the meats to such a fine paste was a real grind. That's why some credit the invention of the meat grinder in 1860 for helping bring hot dogs to a greater market, as it made sausage making infinitely easier. Pushcart vendors brought both cooked and uncooked franks to the neighborhood, the first being non-kosher, as kosher franks weren't readily available until a decade later.

When first produced, hot dogs were encased in natural casing, which would contain the fillers and present that snap when boiled. Some franks were made from all beef and others beef and pork; a third variety was all-beef kosher. Today, the choices are endless, from all natural collagen casings to skinless, cured and uncured, using a variety of meats and poultry.

NO BUN INTENDED

If you've ever eaten a freshly grilled hot dog on a bun, then you need to thank those who originated the concept. Perhaps you're thinking it's Nathan's or Hebrew National, but you'd be wrong. Every time your delicious hot dog lounges snugly in a lightly toasted roll, you have Charles Feltman to thank. He didn't just make New York the capital of the hot dog–loving world, he made Coney Island the epicenter. Feltman arrived in America in 1856 at the age of fifteen with the necessary experience that he gained as a butcher back in Germany. According to Coney Island History Project (CIHP, coneyislandhistory.org), which has immortalized his story, it was in 1867 when Feltman could be seen pushing a pie cart on the beach of Coney Island. He eventually graduated to selling sausages when he had an "aha!" moment to put them on buns. It is presumed that he arrived at this new approach for eating sausage because he was looking for a convenient way for his customers to stroll the beach, hot dog in hand. It also saved precious pennies, as no cutlery or plates were needed. He called his innovation Coney Island red hots and sold them for ten cents. Arthur Schwartz cited a

A bustling Surf Avenue on Brooklyn's Coney Island in 1913 draws crowds to Feltman's pavilion, pictured in the background. *Library of Congress, Prints and Photographs Division.*

"wheelwright" (a person who constructed pushcarts) with helping Feltman design a pushcart that could be heated to accommodate sausages on buns. He was successful and built a wagon for Feltman that had a tin-lined chest to keep the rolls fresh, and he rigged a small charcoal stove inside to boil the sausages. They looked remarkably like the vendor carts we see today. The advent of a subway line that took New Yorkers from city sidewalks to seaside boardwalks was a boon for Feltman. He eventually moved from pushcart vendor to restaurateur and created an empire. CIHP described his holdings on Coney Island, in the spot that would become AstroLand Park:

> *By the early 1900s it covered a full city block and consisted of nine restaurants, a roller coaster, a carousel, a ballroom, an outdoor movie theater, a hotel, a beer garden, a bathhouse, a pavilion, a Tyrolean village, two enormous bars and a maple garden. By the 1920s Feltman's Ocean Pavilion was serving five million customers a year and was billed as the world's largest restaurant.*

Dog Fight

You would think that Feltman would be a household name and toasted every year at your family BBQ. However, in a story you just can't make up, 1916 saw one of Feltman's employees overshadow him. Nathan Handwerker, a Polish immigrant, was working at Feltman's slicing rolls and running dogs to the grilling station. At the time, two of his friends, who were then undiscovered entertainers Jimmy Durante and Eddie Cantor, encouraged

Customers in 1947 converging on the Nathan's stand at the intersection of Stillwell and Surf. *Library of Congress, Prints and Photographs Division.*

Handwerker to strike out on his own. Both worked on Coney Island, Cantor as a singer and Durante as his piano player. The two suggested that by saving his $11-per-week paycheck he could have the funds needed to become his own boss. When he had saved $300, he opened his stand just a few blocks from Feltman's on Stillwell and Surf. He used a spicy recipe developed by his nineteen-year-old bride, Ida, one handed down from her grandmother. You might think as a thank-you for her role that he would name his stand Ida's, but you'd be wrong. He called it Nathan's, and he went on to establish a hot dog empire.

Handwerker was a sharp businessman, and he undercut Feltman's price by half. But because of the cheap price, people were leery of the product, questioning its quality at only a nickel. He reacted quickly, first promoting his product by giving away free root beer and pickles. Then he offered free hot dogs to the doctors and nurses at Coney Island Hospital if they wore their hospital uniforms to the restaurant. He even dressed his employees in white doctor's coats. Handwerker's cronies Durante and Cantor spread the word to their friends, such as Grace Kelly, Lucille Ball and Jackie Gleason. They were all pictured eating and enjoying Nathan's hot dogs, helping cement its image as *the* hot dog of New York. In 1925, vaudeville star Sophie Tucker sang about his franks. When someone suggested that the song made Handwerker famous, the stand was rebranded "Nathan's Famous." Perhaps Nathan's is best known for its annual Fourth of July hot dog eating contest. At the time of this writing, Joey Chestnut had just won his sixteenth contest, downing sixty-three hot dogs, while Miki Sudo won her eighth contest in the women's division devouring an impressive forty. Nathan's Famous restaurants can be found in places as far flung as Kuwait and are the official hot dog of Major League Baseball. Not a bad legacy for a former hot dog bun slicer!

Answering to a Higher Authority

Everything changed back in Manhattan in 1872, when Isaac Gellis and his wife, Sarah, opened a kosher butcher shop on the LES. Within two years, they began selling all-beef kosher versions of what was then still called sausages. Gellis knew a thing or two about meat. Before immigrating to the States, Gellis had been contracted to ship meat from his butcher shop in Berlin to the Union army during the Civil War. On Essex Street, staffed by their seven children, they formed Isaac Gellis Kosher Provisions and became one of the largest purveyors of a variety of meats, most famously their hot dogs and salami. They were the suppliers to many of New York's founding delis, including Katz's, 2nd Avenue and Carnegie. In a crazy coincidence, Eddie Cantor, one of the heroes of the Nathan's story, also worked for Isaac Gellis as a deliveryman. Hasia Diner in her book *Lower East Side Memories* quoted Cantor as saying that he was "the world's supreme delicatessen eater, absorbing more salami, pastrami, bologna and frankfurters in that short span than most families do in a lifetime." The Gellises' marital journey is as interesting as their success once they arrived. Isaac and Sarah wed on the very ship that brought them from Russia to New York. They became pillars of the business community as well as Jewish life on the Lower East Side, as founders of the Eldridge Street Synagogue.

The competition heated up as others began marketing their brand of kosher sausage, and Merwin noted that by the 1930s, there were more than a dozen kosher sausage companies on the Lower East Side, most located near the slaughterhouses where the meat was purchased. The availability of kosher sausage products, not just hot dogs but also salami and bologna, helped fuel the rise of the delicatessen, just as the deli helped propel the purveyors to the next level. So entwined was their reliance on each other than many delis were called *wurst gesheftn*, which means sausage stores.

Gellis was not the only kosher hot dog purveyor to go on to become a leader in the kosher meat industry. You might have heard of a little company called Hebrew National, which answered to a higher authority. Founded in 1905 by Russian immigrant Theodore Krainin, Hebrew National established itself on East Broadway on the LES. By 1921, it had developed a reputation for having not only meat that was kosher certified but also higher than the standards required by law, hence the catchy tagline. The company was bought in 1928 by Isadore Pinckowitz, a Romanian Jewish immigrant. Under the new ownership, Hebrew National opened its own retails stores. Ted Merwin cited a portion of dialogue from a Sholem Aleichem play to illustrate just how widespread the popularity of Hebrew National's hot dogs was. Aleichem's main character, Motl, describes how as an immigrant in New York his brother got a job selling "haht dawgz" for the "Hibru Neshnel Delikatesn." He advises everyone, "If you're hungry, you step into one and order a haht dawg with mustard and horseradish." Hot dogs sound a bit more proper when discussed with a royal British accent, as occurred in 1939. At a picnic he hosted for King George VI and Queen Elizabeth, President Roosevelt served hot dogs and beer. *Smithsonian Magazine*, in reporting the outing, noted that the queen asked the president how to eat a hot dog, and he replied, "Very simple, push it into your mouth and keep pushing until it's gone." Beloved poet Maya Angelou apparently enjoyed her hot dogs with beer as well. She once said, "I love a Hebrew National hot dog with an ice-cold Corona—no lime. If the phone rings, I won't answer until I'm done."

The rapid growth and proliferation of kosher products and certification were not without its share of controversy and scandal. The Orthodox community was not convinced that Hebrew National's kosher certification was kosher enough. Their skepticism about deception in the kosher meat industry was justified, with regard to one company named Jacob Branfman and Son. In 1933, this kosher meat supplier was indicted for selling non-kosher meat, which was "delivered in the dark of night after the mashgiach (Rabbinical supervisor) went home." The high-stakes surveillance of the incident involved a doctor from the Department of Health stationed in an apartment across the way, watching through binoculars as 2,500 pounds of "non-kosher briskets of beef" were seized. Branfman was soon answering to a higher authority as well: Magistrate Jonah J. Goldstein.

Let's Be Frank

Hot dogs have become ubiquitous, as street vendors can be seen selling New York hot dogs throughout the five boroughs. It's reported that the vendor who is positioned outside the Central Park Zoo pays $300,000 a year for that right. Hot dogs have also been seen as a decent wager in sports betting. An unusual tradition started when in 1999 Rudy Giuliani, then mayor of New York, wagered, among other things, Nathan's hot dogs as collateral against the Mets facing the Arizona Diamondbacks. Soon after, he again wagered 240 Nathan's franks on a Little League World Series baseball game. The governor of New York got in on the action in 2003 in a World Series matchup against the Florida Marlins. The Yankees lost the series, and then Governor George Pataki had to turn over Coney Island hot dogs and New York State apples.

Hot dogs have become one of the country's favorite fast foods. According to the National Hot Dog and Sausage Council (NHDSC), here is a run-down of some fast fun facts. Soda wins out over beer to wash down your dog, with mustard just eking out a win over ketchup for topping. However, some diehard hot dog stores won't even offer the red stuff, feeling it's sacrilege to use anything but mustard. Just ask Clint Eastwood's character Dirty Harry, who was quoted as saying, "Nobody, I mean nobody, puts ketchup on a hot dog." A whopping 75 percent of Americans feel that it is unpatriotic to have a summer BBQ without a hot dog on the grill, beating out potato salad and watermelon. As for how to best eat a hot dog, most pray at the shrine of Charles Feltman, with 90 percent saying that a bun is a must. That is, unless you order a New York–only type of oversized hot dog. New Yorkers don't call it knockwurst or a fatty—they call it a "special," as it is nearly two inches thick and is eaten with a fork and knife. Don't try ordering it anywhere else, as they probably won't know what you're talking about. And if you had any doubt that the hot dog is everyone's favorite ballpark food, it is estimated that 19 million were consumed at baseball games in the summer of 2022.

Send a Salami to Your Boy in the Army

When salami and its brother from another mother, bologna, burst onto the scene in New York, it came bearing a European pedigree, most notably Italy, whose word for salt is the basis of the word salami. These fermented

Harry Tarowsky
cradling a Katz's
salami. *Katz's Deli.*

and air-dried sausages have been eaten for centuries. Most of the same companies that produced hot dogs extruded other kosher meats, such as salami and bologna. In New York, that would include Isaac Gellis and Hebrew National and, in the Midwest, the Chicago-based Best Kosher Sausage Company (that's not a testimonial, that's its name), which produces Shofar and Mogen David. Several of these companies have gone head to head to show that their salami is the tastiest, the least fatty and has the best water content. Offering a sagacious settlement that rivals Solomon's ruling, the *New York Times* quoted Leo Steiner of Carnegie Deli: "Salami is salami is salami." While salami was not necessarily the star of the deli counter, it was an ever-present option. In my home, when we had breakfast for dinner, salami and eggs were a favorite. Back in the day, delis would sell the small ends of salami with the catchy phrase "a nickel a *schtickel*" (small bite). Another more well-known phrase also revolved around salami in the 1940s, when Katz's Deli, among others, promoted the patriotic idea to "Send a salami to your boy in the army." The owner's three sons were serving in the military, and when it came to sending an authentic taste of home, salami just made sense, as it was easy to ship and could last for weeks without refrigeration. Katz's trademarked the slogan, and it became another great association with this deli and New York. However, the true origin of the phrase is in question. There's no doubt that Katz's was the standard-bearer for shipping out salami overseas. However, some credit a waiter named Louis Schwartz, who worked at a Midtown deli, for coining the phrase. Additionally, Schwartz was known for his efforts in selling war bonds, raising more than $4 million for the war effort.

You're Taking My Kishkes Out

It might seem a stretch, but kishke—a hard-to-find, old-school deli item—was actually considered a sausage, as it was an encased ground stuffing. Kishke is a combination of grains, veggies, schmaltz (chicken fat) and sometimes meat. This was a true peasant dish, as its real purpose was to use up leftovers. The stuffing would be filled into a casing made from a cow's intestine, hence its name kishke, which means intestine in Yiddish. It's certainly not a compliment when you tell someone they're taking your kishkes out, as it means they're causing you undo agita. This is a dish that you shouldn't knock until you've tried it. Probably, the only place to do that would be a New York deli, where it often goes by the name stuffed derma. Rest assured, most today use synthetic casings or bake it free form. It makes a delicious side dish, especially when topped with a rich brown gravy. It's Thanksgiving stuffing and eastern European resourcefulness rolled up in one.

As long as we're talking foods that are stuffed, it would be a slight not mention the king of stuffed Jewish food found in every deli throughout New York: the stuffed cabbage. The countries that lay claim to these cabbage rolls are about as numerous as flavors of ice creams, but it is the eastern European variety most commonly served up in American Jewish delicatessens and restaurants. The cabbage leaves are softened and then filled with a ground beef mixed with rice and topped with a tomatoey sauce. The sweet-and-sour balance depends on the country of origin. This time-intensive labor of love was associated with the Jewish autumnal holidays, most specifically Sukkot and Simchat Torah. In her book *Jewish Cooking in America*, Joan Nathan noted that this tradition symbolizes "the desire for plenty during the harvest period." Even the *Settlement Cookbook*, one of the first Jewish-focused American cookbooks written in 1901, contains a recipe for stuffed cabbage. Gil Marks noted that it has been around for more than two thousand, years and it's still being enjoyed in New York as an iconic deli offering.

~~~

Kishke

1 small onion, chopped
1 carrot, peeled and cut into bite-size pieces
1 celery rib, cut into bite-size pieces

Don't forget the gravy—it takes kishke to the next level of deliciousness. *Stu Spivack @Flickr.*

1 clove of garlic
¾ cup all-purpose flour
½ cup matzo meal
6 tablespoons chicken fat (or neutral vegetable oil)
1½ teaspoons kosher salt
½ teaspoon black pepper
½ teaspoon paprika
¼ teaspoon garlic powder

Tear a sheet of aluminum foil 18 inches long and top with a piece of parchment paper, slightly smaller at each end.

Place all the ingredients in a food processor fitted with the metal blade. Process until the mixture is thick like cookie dough. Place the bowl in the fridge to chill and preheat the oven to 425°F.

When the oven reaches temperature, turn the stuffing out onto the parchment paper and form a 2-inch-wide log. Roll the log up in the papers and seal the ends by twisting the foil closed—it should look like a Tootsie Roll.

Bake for 30 minutes, reduce the temperature to 350°F and bake an additional 30 minutes. Unwrap and cook 10 minutes longer to brown. Slice with a serrated knife and serve warm as a side dish. It's especially delicious when topped with gravy.

I'LL DRINK TO THAT

FROM EGG CREAMS TO WINE

*Y*ou'd be hard pressed to find someone anywhere other than in New York experienced in making a classic New York egg cream. Leave New York City and you might be asked, "Dr. Brown? Who is she, a surgeon?" Few would know the true taste of pure New York seltzer or find bottles of Manischewitz on the store's shelf, year-round. That's because those beverages are not just from New York—they are part of New York, where the iconic egg cream was born, Dr. Brown's became a deli favorite, seltzer was delivered by a local peddler and Manischewitz was not just a Jewish favorite. Here's a toast to the beverages that call New York home.

No Egg, No Cream

The egg cream might be not only New York's most iconic drink but the coolest as well. Brooklyn-born Jewish music legend Lou Reed took time away from writing hits like "Walk on the Wild Side" to write a little ditty he called "Egg Cream":

> *When I was a young man, no bigger than this*
> *A chocolate egg-cream was not to be missed*
> *Some U-Bet's chocolate syrup, seltzer water mixed with milk*
> *You stir it up into a heady fro, tasted just like silk*

A 1911 flyer distributed by *National Druggist* suggests preparation for a variety of drinks, including the iconic egg cream. *Lucky Dog, Wikimedia Commons.*

Lou Reed sang you the formula, but he doesn't explain how a drink with no egg and usually no cream became known as an egg cream. As with so many of the foods we've discussed, there's more than one theory about its derivation. It could be an interpretation of the phrase *echt keem*, which in Yiddish means pure sweetness, or a twist on the French "chocolate et crème," a drink that New York Yiddish theater star Boris Thomashevsky tasted in France and wanted to enjoy back home. It might have derived from the frothy foam that looks like whipped egg whites and is the crowning glory of the drink. The first report of an egg cream–like drink debuting in New York was in the 1880s, according to Andrew F. Smith, when raw eggs were mixed into soda water along with chocolate syrup and cream. That concoction was most likely the expensive version of what became an inexpensive drink for the masses.

Substituting milk for the cream and omitting the egg, you sacrificed a little richness and decadence, but you made the drink more affordable—so much so that it was the darling of soda fountains, drugstores and luncheonettes throughout New York at the start of the twentieth century. Elliot Willensky, in his book *When Brooklyn Was the World, 1920–1957*, aptly wrote that "a candy store minus an egg cream, in Brooklyn at least, was as difficult to conceive of as the Earth without gravity."

The version of the egg cream that shot to meteoric popularity takes three arms to make—one to hold the glass, one to stir the milk and one to squirt the seltzer. The version that became the standard was most likely the brainchild of Louis Auster, who owned a candy store on the Lower East Side. It is said that Auster experimented with a few different combinations of syrups, eventually creating his own, which he mixed with milk and seltzer from siphon bottles. It was a winner. He charged a whopping three cents for the drink and kept the formula a secret. The website What's Cooking America reports on a legend that Auster was offered money for his formula

Lexington Candy Shop on the UES still makes egg creams the old-fashioned way. *Photo by author.*

from a national ice cream chain but refused to sell his recipe. Upon turning them down, the buyers called him anti-Semitic slurs, which is when Auster vowed to take the formula with him to his grave, which he did. Vanilla and coffee egg creams became popular flavors in the 1950s, but sadly, by the late 1900s, the drink had begun to fall out of favor.

Luckily, there are still shops in New York City making an egg cream the old-fashioned way. Lexington Candy Shop, owned and operated by the Philis family on the corner of Lexington and 83rd Street, has been doing it since 1925. John Philis, the grandson of the original Greek owner, gave me a demonstration in making this iconic drink. First, they add the chocolate syrup, which they make themselves, much as Auster did. John, however, was happy to share the recipe of combining three ingredients: water, cocoa and lots of sugar. John says they make their own "because it has no preservatives and hits just the right sweetness." They break form by using half and half in place of whole milk, to give the drink extra body and taste. He agrees that without a soda fountain spigot, you would need three hands to mix the drink vigorously to create the proper foam. He notes that the key to a perfect egg cream is "cold seltzer from 'the jerk,'" the spigot that dispenses carbonated beverages. If you ever wondered how the term soda jerk evolved, now you know. While I was there, a family from New Orleans was taste testing every flavor the luncheonette offered and voted chocolate the definitive winner.

Unless a shop made its own, there was and still is only one chocolate syrup synonymous with a New York egg cream: Fox's U-Bet. It was born at the turn of the century in Brooklyn, and from the day it took its first squeeze, it was the only bottled syrup any true egg cream maker would use. Invented by Herman and Ida Fox, in the early 1900s U-Bet could be found on the shelves in every store with a soda fountain. The syrup might have been favored because it has a less sweet and more milk chocolate flavor. No magic with branding here—the same yellow and red labels from the original glass bottles can still be found on the plastic bottles today. Why the name, you ask? Herman just liked the phrase U-Bet, and it stuck.

2 Cents Plain

Seltzer is not only iconic in New York as the crowning glory of an egg cream—it was a beverage in its own right. While New York did not invent it, it certainly can claim ownership for popularizing it. You might recall (I didn't) from high school chemistry class that Joseph Priestly gave water its bubbles when he infused it with carbon dioxide. However, it was not a widely consumed beverage until, as Smith reported, it was improvised in New York. When sugar prices increased, Jewish soda manufacturers needed to produce a beverage that was refreshing and inexpensive. Carbonating water to create seltzer fit the bill. Seltzer was not new to eastern Europeans—in fact, the word *seltzer* is derived from a German town called Selters, located in the state of Hesse at the Tanus Mountains. The area was known for its natural mineral springs, and our current-day seltzer borrows its name from that region. By 1907, New York boasted more than one hundred seltzer manufacturers, which were selling what became known as "workman's champagne."

Peddlers across the LES would carry crates filled with seltzer bottles generally ten to a case, as home deliveries of seltzer were as much a part of the New York experience as the milkman bringing fresh eggs and milk. The deliveryman would go to what was known as a filling station, where the iconic siphon bottles would be filled with sparkling seltzer water. Alex Gomberg gave me a crash course in everything New York seltzer, and he should know, as the great-grandson of Mo Gomberg, who established Gomberg Seltzer Works in 1953. Gomberg is the last remaining seltzer factory in New York and is still housed in Canarsie, Brooklyn, where it began. Today, Gomberg, along with his father and uncle, are known as the Brooklyn Seltzer Boys. They use original Czechoslovakian and Austrian blue, green and clear hand-blown bottles that date back to the 1800s. The antique bottles are filled in a century-old siphon filler with triple-filtered New York tap. The water is chilled to forty-three degrees and then forced under pressure into a six-head siphon. Gomberg, proud to carry on this family tradition, told me, "We're the only ones still standing—we're a living memory."

At the local soda shop in the early 1900s, clear unadulterated seltzer water would cost what became a colloquial term for the drink: "2 cents plain." Move forward a few decades and seltzer sales declined, as the next generation were taking to more Americanized drinks, like cola. But an "aha" moment came when Canada Dry began marketing its flavored bubbly water to a new demographic of consumers. At first, it wanted to call its drinks flavored seltzer,

Seltzer siphon bottles were almost always delivered ten to a case. *Tom Bentz, Flickr.*

but it quickly learned that seltzer was a New York term and not recognizable to most of the country. It rebranded its version sparkling water. By the late 1900s, the FDA had to regulate the product, differentiating between the various sparkling waters. Here's a quick tutorial: seltzer is carbonated water, no minerals added; club soda is carbonated water, minerals added, including sodium; sparkling mineral water is naturally carbonated generally from a well or spring; and tonic water is carbonated water with minerals added, as well as quinine to add bitterness. If you're looking for a taste from the old country, reach for a siphon or can of cold plain seltzer. No salt, no preservatives, no calories—no equal.

IS THERE A DOCTOR IN THE HOUSE?

When you think of the perfect soft drink to wash down your towering mound of pastrami, I'm sure that a soda with a hint of celery is exactly what you were craving. It would have been had you lived in New York in 1868, when Dr. Brown's Celery Tonic debuted. Its association with the city and most specifically Jewish deli food has remained ever since. The soda was first bottled in 1886 on Water Street in Manhattan and was touted by Dr. Brown's as being a true tonic with health benefits. The flavor is reminiscent of a peppery, slightly sweet celery-tinged ginger ale, which is achieved by crushed celery seeds. The drink was the perfect tonic to cut through the fatty deli foods. David Sax in *Tastemakers* pointed out that celery-infused soda was not a stretch for Jewish immigrants arriving in New York. He noted that in Poland and Ukraine, many worked in sugar-related industries, so "working with soda was a natural extension, and celery was a flavor they knew well from the old country." You might recall from an earlier reference that seltzer was considered the "workman's champagne." Apparently, Cel-Ray (its new name, once the FDA said it cannot be called a tonic, with medicinal overtones) was dubbed "Jewish champagne," and along with cream soda it was one of the two most popular flavors.

As for Dr. Brown, Harry Gold, marketing director for the brand, told an *LA Times* reporter back in 1986:

> For generation to generation, we've been told there was a doctor by that name who invented cream soda and celery tonic now known as Cel-Ray.... But we have no records that tell us anything about the good doctor. It's like a biblical story. We accept it on faith.

Not so, says Marianne Santora, who is familiar with the folklore, as she supports the existence of an actual Dr. Brown saying, "He made tonics for the people, including a celery tonic that was thought to be good for calming stomachs and bowels." According to Santora, the carbonation was added to make it more palatable. There's actual science behind that concept, as the bubbles stimulate taste, create a refreshing sensation and carry the drink's aroma to activate your sense of smell. Dr. Brown's was decidedly a New York beverage, so much so that today various iconic New York images appear on its bottles and cans to reinforce its New York roots. The Statue of Liberty is on its cream soda, the most popular flavor, followed by black cherry, which bears the Central Park Carousel on its

Who says you can't elevate a Cel-Ray soda? *Creativemariolorek, Adobe Stock.*

label. A not-to-be-ignored root beer features a New York ice cream parlor, as it's particularly good as the base for a root beer float. Cel-Ray, which features the Brooklyn Bridge on its label, still has a following. What started as a New York soda with a Jewish identity is now a national brand, and it's still the choice of delis across the country.

THE GLASS WAS HALF FULL

Jewish immigrants had a drinking problem that was complex and intertwined with establishing their status as Americans. On the one hand, drinking was a common practice in America, but Jewish people who reserved their alcohol consumption to holidays and Shabbat were just not seen as regular folk. Marni Davis, who literally wrote the book on the topic, called *Jews and Booze*, noted the uneasy balance between assimilating fully and maintaining Jewish identity. For Jewish immigrants, their relationship with alcohol was a defining feature of this see-saw they found themselves on. At the onset of their arrival, Jewish businesses produced and sold alcoholic beverages, and that was one way to affirm their true Americanization while remaining, as Davis noted, "meaningfully Jewish." Throughout history, the Jewish community was integral in beer brewing, as brokers for wine producers and creating markets for alcoholic beverages. They brought that expertise with them to America and, in some form or another, practiced this trade where they settled.

It's hard to analyze real data to determine how enmeshed the Jewish immigrants were in the New York drinking scene, as census data related to businesses accounted for lots of factors, but not religious affiliation. But make no mistake, there were plenty of Jewish saloonkeepers, brewers and vintners in New York. Much like the deli, the Jewish saloon was as much a place to grab a *schnapps* (a cloyingly sweet peach drink) as it was to exchange ideas and feel comfortable among their own. Davis painted a picture of the bars they established feeling more like cafés, with tables and chairs, restaurant style. It didn't take long for the reputation of these saloons to become suspect, and many thought that they were seeded in moral delinquency and responsible for criminal activity. The Jewish bars became known as the "Jew saloon" and were viewed as "primary perpetrators of vice in New York." A 1908 report released by New York City's chief of police claimed that the overwhelming majority of the city's criminals were mostly Polish and Russian Jews, as well as southern Italians.

Saloons were not the only enterprises managed by Jewish immigrants. As far back as 1855, Samuel Liebmann from Württemberg, Germany, made his mark as a premier beer brewer. He settled in Bushwick and established an operation on what Davis called "Brewers' Row." There in the 1880s, he began brewing Rheingold Beer, a nationally recognized brand for decades to follow. Who doesn't associate Rheingold beer with New York? A hot dog in one hand and a Rheingold beer in the other. While the brewery declined in the 1950s, it made its mark indelibly in New York.

Wine was also a big component of the Jewish immigrant foray into alcohol. Sam Schapiro, an immigrant from the Galicia region of what is now Poland, produced sacramental wine. Schapiro Kosher Wine dates back to 1899 to a plant located underneath Rivington Street. Sam was once quoted as saying that the wine was so thick you could "cut it with a knife." The winery remained there for more than one hundred years and was the oldest kosher winery in New York. Not to be outdone, the Herzogs cemented the LES as the kosher Napa Valley. Their royal beginnings started in Slovakia in the early 1800s. Family patriarch Philip Herzog produced wine for Emperor Franz-Josef, who dubbed Philip a baron and decreed that they would be the wine producers for the royal court. In the 1930s, when the region was overrun by Nazis, Philip's grandson Eugene and his family survived in hiding. His parents were not as fortunate and perished in Auschwitz. Fleeing Slovakia in 1948, Eugene arrived with his family in New York City and began working for New York's Royal Wine Company. He rose from truck driver to winemaker to sales manager and became the majority shareholder, having been paid in stock. In 1958, he bought the winery and called it Kedem. The family used grape juice instead of sugar to sweeten New York's Concord grapes. They became not only a driving force in the kosher wine world but also the inventor of kosher grape juice, which according to Kedem is the top-selling kosher product in the United States.

This brings us to the big name in New York wine: Manischewitz. If cough syrup and red wine had a baby, it would be called Manischewitz wine. If you've never tried it, you should. It has notes of…oh, who are we kidding? It is not rated on *Wine Enthusiast*, its vintage is yesterday and twist cap is how it was meant to be opened. But it has a singular taste and an association with Jewish culture that began in New York. Its trajectory is what legends are made of, and its customer base might be surprising. What we know as Manischewitz wine is really a wine produced by the Monarch Wine Company. Back in the 1930s, Monarch started producing this syrupy-sweet wine from New York's Concord grapes, which can be bitter, hence the copious amount of added sugar. Initially, the company was based in Manhattan, but in 1939 it moved to sprawling facility at Bush Terminal in Brooklyn. There it began producing enough wine to fill Passover glasses all the way to California. It created a boon for the borough and immense success for the company. In the 1940s, to give its company more recognizable branding, it struck a licensing deal with the Manischewitz food company. That's right, Manischewitz has never actually produced a single drop of wine—it just licensed its name to its New York producer, Monarch.

Kosher wines were pivotal to the problematic culture of drinking during Prohibition. In 1920, the Eighteenth Amendment, with its follow-up Volstead Act giving it teeth, placed the Jewish immigrants in a precarious situation. Davis explained, "Jews' economic practices and cultural attitudes now came into direct conflict with the nation's prevailing moral and political ideals, and with American law as well." Like so many issues the Jewish immigrants faced, due to sheer numbers, New York became a central hub for this debate. On the one hand, you have a thriving form of commerce that helped the Jews appear to be very American in their practices both socially and economically, and then you had laws that were restricting both. Jews began internally quibbling and disagreeing on how to navigate the thirteen years that Prohibition prevailed. An outgrowth was the Jewish bootlegger. There was a catch-22 that many seized: a provision to the Eighteenth Amendment allowed the selling of sacramental wine. The offshoot of that was a deep dive by many industrious and unscrupulous Jewish merchants to use that act as a back door to bootlegging. Arnold Rothstein, whom you might remember from a previous chapter as the gangster who operated out of Reuben's Restaurant, was also the financier for Waxey Gordon. Waxey operated out of the Lower East Side and ran a smuggling operation along with Maxie Greenberg of St. Louis. I suppose your names had to rhyme to be part of this Jewish syndicate. Jewish wine stores popped up in every Jewish neighborhood, selling sacramental wine, or at least that's what it was supposed to be used for. It was even rumored that Schapiro's winery not only filled the orders of local rabbis, but also in the back "he had the juice." One of the leading bootleggers was Jewish criminal Dutch Schultz, who operated out of the Bronx, providing untold gallons of bootlegged alcohol to the neighborhood.

Every good story has villains and heroes, and New York during Prohibition was no different. However, the unlikely hero during Prohibition was of dubious stature both literally and figuratively. Enter Izzy Einstein, who Davis wrote was a Prohibition agent focused on New York's illicit bootleggers. Izzy was an unlikely fed, short and a bit pudgy, who argued that his atypical looks would be to his advantage. This Austrian immigrant convinced the bureau that "he would never be spotted as a sleuth." Along with his partner, Moe Smith, they made 4,392 arrests in five years. One time he convinced a bartender at a Midtown club that he was a rabbi, and at another spot he ate a ham sandwich to prove that he was not Jewish and there to bust them. He was responsible for taking down Dutch Schultz's Harlem enterprise, confiscating "$35,000 worth of 'sacramental Dubonnet'" and in 1921 raided Menorah Wine Company in downtown New York for selling wine without the proper permits. Eventually, the sacramental wine business began to dry up as crackdowns became more prevalent.

After Prohibition ended, kosher wines were still viewed as being a religious drink, hence the original Manischewitz bottle with a bearded rabbi gracing the label. Roger Horowitz wrote in his book *Kosher USA* that the wine was marketed to Jewish New Yorkers almost exclusively for the holidays. But then a trend was observed. The wine sales peaked at Christmas and Thanksgiving; even "a relatively minor occasion as St. Patrick's Day causes a discernible rise." The reality was that nearly 85 percent of those

Top: Official documents for Isidor "Izzy" Einstein issued by the Treasury Department and the Internal Revenue Service in 1920. *Wikimedia Commons.*

Bottom: Official documents for Moe W. Smith, who partnered with Izzy Einstein. *Wikimedia Commons.*

purchasing Manischewitz wine were not Jewish. The wine was appealing to Gentile consumers, more specifically African Americans. After the Second World War, many African Americans migrated from the South and settled in New York City, where they lived and worked in communities alongside their Jewish neighbors. They began purchasing the wine in the local stores, and it soon became their go-to brand, as its sweetness was reminiscent of southern wines they enjoyed. Ad campaigns recognized this trend and featured Black musicians such as Lionel Hampton, who touted "Manischewitz kosher wine harmonizes with us sweetly!" Their marketing resulted in Sammy Davis Jr. singing the wine's praises. He was a perfect choice to hawk Manischewitz, as he was a well-liked celebrity, African American and someone who had converted to Judaism—the spokesman trifecta for this product. According to Horowitz, New York had promoted and produced the "first true crossover Jewish food product in American history." One might say that Manischewitz is out of this world, as it's reported that astronaut Buzz Aldrin during a lunar landing exclaimed "Man-O-Manischewitz." He blurted out the company's slogan that was so popular at the time. The wine went from a post-Prohibition Brooklyn-born sacred wine to a pop culture symbol. Let's drink to that!

~~~

New York Egg Cream

Three ingredients, three hands, three seconds.

Spoon 2 tablespoons of chocolate syrup (U-Bet recommended) in a large glass. Add ¼ cup cold milk (whole will be richer, but you can use low or no fat). Tilt the glass and begin pouring very cold seltzer into the glass, stirring vigorously as you do, until the froth reaches the top.

SWEET TOOTH

COOKIES, CAKE AND CANDY

Beser dem beker vie dem dokter.
("Better to give to the baker than the doctor.")

New Yorkers weren't born with a silver spoon in their mouth—they were born with a dessert fork. Their love affair with deli and appetizing can only be matched by their devotion to dessert. New Yorkers come by their sweet tooth naturally, as the regions from where many emigrated were known for their sweet treats. After the arrival of the great waves of immigrants, German, Polish, Hungarian and Czech bakeries sprang up across the city, from the lower tip of Manhattan to the Upper East Side in Yorkville, throughout Brooklyn, Queens and the Bronx. These bakers honed their craft and satiated the sugar cravings of the new immigrants. Several of their specialties began to develop a cult following and a Jewish association. Just like yeast in dough, they rose above the others. I'm referring to the harmoniously frosted black and white cookie, twisty rugelach, swirled babka and creamy cheesecake. Additionally, New York experienced a candy frenzy as confectionery stores proliferated in Jewish neighborhoods and candy-makers thrived. These sweet treats have satisfied a city and have been synonymous with New York for more than one hundred years.

What's Black and White and Eaten All Over

There is nothing inherently Jewish about the black and white cookie, which makes its association with Jewish culture an enigma. Ironically, this iconic New York cookie less arrived and more derived from German (probably non-Jewish) immigrants who made their way to Utica, in Upstate New York. There, at Hemstrought's Bakery, the "half-moon" was created. It became an instant hit and traveled downstate to every bakery in the city. Once it did, it was featured front and center in the bakery window garnering the spotlight. As *New York Times* food columnist Melissa Clarke's noted, "These cookies are not only a New York staple but also an essential component of Jewish culture.... Black and whites have been an entrenched part of the very robust Jewish cookie scene in New York for a century." Additionally, some don't even know to what category

The original building that housed Glaser's Bakery in the Yorkville section of the UES. *Herb Glaser.*

of dessert it belongs. Basically, it's a drop cake masquerading as a cookie and has often been the subject of ridicule and suspicion. Food journalist Molly O' Neill lamented the black and white cookie's existence as "a broken promise" and called them "floury cakes baked in a cookie style." Not so sure what's wrong with that, but criticism and skepticism aside, it has survived more than a century of scrutiny and remains the symbolic cookie of New York with a strong Jewish identity.

You know you've reached iconic New York status and national recognition when you are the subject of a *Seinfeld* episode. Such was the case for the black and white cookie when it starred alongside the chocolate and cinnamon babka on episode 77, during the sixth season of *Seinfeld*. In "The Dinner Party," it was agreed that Elaine and Jerry would go to their local bakery and purchase dessert for an evening with friends. After eying them while waiting on line, Jerry couldn't resist ordering a black and white cookie. He theorized:

> *The thing about eating a black and white cookie, Elaine, is you want to get some black and some white in each bite. Nothing mixes better than vanilla*

These Zaro black and white cookies are in mid-production, waiting for the vanilla icing to set before adding the chocolate. *Photo by author.*

*and chocolate, and yet somehow racial harmony eludes us. If people would
only look to the cookie, all our problems would be solved.*

Elaine mocks his sociological perspective, but Jerry insists and reiterates,
"Look to the cookie." One thing the show confirmed was that in 1994, when

the episode aired, the black and white cookie, with its ying-yang frosting, was firmly a New York institution ready for primetime. The morning after proved to be quite the day for Herb Glaser at his family's landmark Glaser's Bakery, a Yorkville institution for 116 years. That morning, Herb's phone rang off the hook. He relayed to me that calls came in from across the country asking if they could ship New York's famous cookie. To appreciate the black and white, you need to taste one fresh from the oven, with a frosting just sweet enough to stand up to the cake-like dough. That's where Zaro's Bakery comes in, founded in 1927 by Yussel Zarobchyk. You know it takes the black and white seriously when you see the cookie painted on its delivery trucks. Its status as premier purveyors of New York sweets came in the late '70s, when it took the leap from being a Bronx institution to becoming the bakery to the world of commuters in Grand Central Station. In its commissary in the Bronx, as well as an underground bakery below the station, it fueled commuters with fresh-baked challah, rugelach and the famous black and whites. Watching the skilled bakers glaze the cookies on my tour with fourth-generation family member Michael Zaro was a sugar rush. They must be doing it right, as annually they sell close to half a billion of this classic New York cookie. If you want the true taste experience of eating what President Obama once called the "unity cookie," don't settle for a sad imitation—you can still find bakery-fresh authentic ones throughout the city.

Twisted Sisters

Some might say that babka was created to provide a vehicle for ingesting obscene amounts of chocolate or cinnamon. Others feel that it was created as a counterpart to the German coffeecake. Whichever assertion is correct, it's irrelevant, as nothing melts in your mouth with layers of yeasty goodness swirled with delicious flavors more than a freshly baked babka. In Polish, the word *babka* means grandmother, so it is no surprise that it is a comforting, hearty, complex cake. If you wonder why your grandmother might have been cranky after making this traditional loaf, it is because it is a laborious task creating the layers of dough with the various fillings and streusel topping. It can involve up to fourteen steps and hours of work, but that is not how it started. Gil Marks traced the history of babka to the early 1800s, when in an effort not to waste anything, the frugal Jewish homemaker would use her extra challah dough, slather it in jam or cinnamon, roll it up and bake it. This custom of filling dough was transformed by bakers in America into the present-day treat we enjoy. Babka has become an artisanal creation, bathed in butter, filled to the point of bursting and sold in the trendiest bakeries in the city.

Chances are that when you buy a packaged babka in New York City, you will be digging into one baked by Green's Bakery. I had the pleasure of speaking to Ben Green, third-generation owner of this legendary Brooklyn-based bakery. Green told me that this bastion of babka produces about four to five thousand loaves per day, six days a week. It produces its babka with the original recipe of his great-grandmother Chana Green, a Holocaust survivor who arrived in New York from Hungary in 1948. Chana first produced the loaves, which only comes in two flavors, chocolate and cinnamon, from her kitchen on the LES. When demand increased and she "wanted to share the love," she began making them from the basement of her son-in-law's restaurant. At that time, this bread-cake hybrid was called *kokosh*, Hungarian for cocoa. When they could no longer operate without a full-fledged bakery, they moved to their present location in the Bed-Stuy section of Brooklyn. Ben said that chocolate remains the most popular, but not by a lot, about 60:40 to the cinnamon, which by the way got some love in the aforementioned *Seinfeld* episode. In finding out that the chocolate babka of their dreams had sold out, Jerry and Elaine were forced to accept what Elaine deemed a "lesser babka," the cinnamon version. Jerry quickly comes to the defense of the cinnamon loaf, saying, "Cinnamon takes a back seat to no babka. People love cinnamon. It should be on tables at restaurants along with salt and pepper."

Green's and almost every New York City bakery with an eastern European background bake babka's sister, rugelach, which literally translates from the Yiddish to mean "little twists." It is a surprising cookie, as so much can be packed into this small croissant-shaped dough. It's no coincidence, then, that rugelach first made its debut in 1683, about the same time as the croissant. Gil Marks provided insight into how these intricate little bites evolved. Jewish leaders in the Austro-Hungarian empire encouraged the community to channel their anger at the brutal Turks and bake these cookies in the crescent shape of the Ottoman war flags. They would then devour the cookie as a "take that" victory, much like Jews eat Hamantaschen during Purim as an edible gesture of defiance against Haman. Marks noted that while the cookies that were developed with the influx of immigrants to New York resembled those early versions, they are decidedly different than what was and is prepared currently in Europe and Israel. It's the addition of cream cheese that differentiates the American immigrant rugelach. Generally, those prepared here also omit yeast, so the resulting cookie is denser and less light and airy. The fillings can vary, too, from chocolate and cinnamon

Zaro's chocolate rugelach wait patiently to be boxed and sent to customers nationwide.
Photo by author.

to jam filled with lots of raisins and nuts. It's a non-holiday-driven bite and available in every New York bakery, not just as an homage to those creative bakers from the 1600s but also because they are so darn good.

Smile, Say Cheesecake

Whether you order it Des Moines, Detroit or DeKalb Avenue in Brooklyn, that creamy confection that appears on more menus than any other dessert is known as New York cheesecake. That's for good reason. The version most Americans enjoy was created in New York City with influences from Ashkenazi immigrants. Much like the black and white cookie, there is nothing historic connecting Jewish people and cheesecake, but it was popularized in Jewish restaurants and the association stuck. It got its start well before, as Marks noted, as early as the fifth century BC, when ancient Greeks were pounding patties of fresh cheese to create a crude version of the dessert. It's said that a form of cheesecake was served at the very first Olympics nearly three thousand years ago. Flash forward to the nineteenth century and the discovery of cream cheese in New York, when everything changed. Ricotta or pot cheese was no longer the go-to fat, and pie crust was replaced by cracker or cake bottoms. New York cheesecake was born, and it became the most popular dessert in every restaurant.

Alan Rosen, who should know a thing or two million about cheesecakes as a third-generation proprietor of Junior's, told me how his grandfather Harry came upon the recipe that would become the restaurant's signature dessert. The story begins like so many others, when Harry Rosen immigrated to New York in 1904 and settled on the Lower East Side. Having first worked as a soda jerk, he opened a sandwich shop in Manhattan. By the 1930s, he owned four more shops but sold them to focus on the one in Brooklyn, where Junior's is situated currently, at the intersection of Fulton Street, DeKalb and Flatbush Avenues. Alan recounted how Harry and their head baker, Eigel Petersen, went around town sampling and buying cheesecakes from every restaurant that served it. They dissected each to discover what attributes they liked best, and from that trial and error, as Alan says, "They hit upon a formula that hasn't changed in seventy-two years. Cream cheese, heavy cream, sugar, fresh eggs and vanilla on a sponge cake base." There must be something to their recipe, as they sell millions per year and are consistently voted by New Yorkers as the champions of cheesecake. When asked what the allure of cheesecake is, quite simply, Alan says, "It's comfort food in its

Postcard image of Lindy's circa 1960s, when it was a New York institution known for its cheesecake. *Bertil Carlson, Wikimedia Commons.*

truest form. It's not fussed up, it's very simple, but you have to be committed to the ingredients, the process and have patience."

When it comes to New York cheesecake, we must mention Lindy's, the famed establishment of Leo Lindemann. Lindy's is no longer operating, but when it did, in its heyday it was the place to be seen and eat cheesecake. What was once a Jewish deli, opened in 1921 by Clara and Leo "Lindy," became a local attraction for columnists, aspiring actors and New Yorkers of all backgrounds. Harpo Marx was a frequent customer and was quoted as saying, "I had a home again…the cheesecake was ambrosia."

Lindy's history was something out of a Damon Runyon story, which is fitting as it was Runyon who popularized and immortalized the restaurant. In many of his stories, including *Guys and Dolls*, the name Lindy's was changed to Mindy's. It was the subject of several stories, the most memorable being a musical number between protagonist Sky Masterson and Nathan Detroit. Masterson was a big fan of Mindy's cheesecake and placed a wager based on Mindy's cheesecake sales. The gangster scenario played out in real life when Jewish mobster Arnold Rothstein, who called Lindy's his "office," received a phone call at the restaurant and was gunned down later that day. Speaking of *Guys and Dolls*, Burt Rapoport, of Rapoport's dairy restaurant, has a story that could have been part of the script. Burt recalled that sometime in the late 1930s, his grandfather brought over a Swedish pastry chef who carried with him a recipe for luscious cheesecake. Harry put it on the menu, and it became their best-selling item. Corporate espionage was in full force when Burt says a competitor approached this Swedish chef at a racetrack. Known for his gambling problem, the chef was offered a fair sum of money in exchange for the cheesecake recipe. From then on, Burt said, their competitor was selling Rapoport's cheesecake.

Sweet Spot

Four out of five dentists might feel that we've more than covered the sweet treats that are synonymous with New York City, but the fifth would not want us to exclude one more entry: candy. The connection between Jews and chocolate dates back centuries to when Jews fleeing the inquisition in Spain found refuge in France. There they are credited with pioneering the development of chocolate. Back in the old country, Jews were involved in beet processing and became integral to sugar production. Put these factors together and it's no surprise that New York became the home to some of the most successful candy-making pioneers. One such confectioner was Stephen Klein, an Austrian candymaker who arrived in New York in 1938. "When I came to this country, I was surprised to see how candy was sold here," he told Morris Friedman, a writer for *Commentary*, in 1952, "I saw that a better, tastier, a more different candy had to be made....I know what chocolates to blend, how to control taste....All the pieces should look good—no *chazerei*," or junk. Klein began as a humble peddler, making candy at night in the kitchen of his apartment and peddling them during the day. He apparently did know how to make a better candy, and he sold them in his New York stores that he called Barton's Bonbonniere. By the time the company changed hands, it had three thousand outlets and a factory in Brooklyn that took up a square block. Klein became a New York candy-making legend, with chorus line dancers marking his Herald Square Store opening and the New York City Board of Transportation granting him special dispensation to open a coveted concession stand in Grand Central Terminal, despite the fact it would be closed on the Sabbath.

Moving down the path on New York's version of Candy Land is taffy. This chewy treat is often associated with the boardwalk in Atlantic City, but it began on a different boardwalk one state over. It was the concoction of Austrian immigrant Herman Herer, who created the candy on Coney Island in 1912. He added too many egg whites to a batch of marshmallow he was making and accidentally created taffy. Albert Bonomo, a Sephardic immigrant who emigrated from Turkey to Brooklyn in 1892, also began selling his version of taffy on Coney Island. He produced both candy and ice cream on the first floor of his home, with his workers living above on the third floor. In 1936, Bonomo bought out Herer's business and rebranded the candy Bonomo Turkish Taffy. Every time you slap a stick of taffy against the table, you have two industrious immigrants to thank.

You can also thank New York for giving rise to Bazooka bubblegum. Bazooka was the creation of Topps Chewing Gum, a business controlled by Morris Chigorinsky, who emigrated from Russia to New York in 1891. Its product, according to the Topps Archives, took a circuitous route, as Chigorinsky was first involved in the American Leaf Tobacco Company. Seems like a leap, but after World War I, the tobacco connection began to wane, and the family established Topps, shifting the focus to chewing gum. Bazooka was known for its super-pink color (hence the reference to bubblegum pink) and those tiny comics that were added in 1947. The family was considered royalty in Crown Heights as both the manufactures of chewing gum and cigars—go figure.

Speaking of chewy, we need to acknowledge Leo Hirschfield, who gave us the Tootsie Roll. Hirschfield immigrated to New York from Austria in 1896 and developed the candy in 1907, named to honor his daughter Clara, whose nickname was "Tootsie." They were the first penny candy to be individually wrapped, not just in New York but anywhere in the country. In a meant-to-be moment, the man who invented the "Born Sucker Machine," which inserted sticks into lollipops, immigrated to New York at the same time as Hirschfield. Sam Born came to New York from Russia in 1910 and by 1916 had created the technology that transformed the Tootsie Roll into the Tootsie Pop. Born went on to create a variety of candies such as Mike and Ike and Peeps.

New York sweet treats found a home then and now at Economy Candy, where a penny could buy you almost any treat. This spot started as a pushcart outside a shoe and hat repair shop on the Lower East Side. According to family members, Morris "Moishe" Cohen would stand outside peddling candy and sacks of fruits and nuts, rain or shine, hot or cold. During the Depression, the shop owners found that the cart was bringing in more revenue than the actual store and made the business decision to shift focus. When Morris and his brother returned from the war, they expanded the store into what still thrives today. One of their specialties then and now is the wide selection of halvah, so much so that it was prominently featured on their original awning. Halvah was a staple of both the appetizing and candy store. Scholars continue to debate who truly created halvah, a sesame confection whose name means sweet in Arabic. It has a crumbly texture and a chalkiness that melts in your mouth. Nevin Martell, in his article "Open Sesame: The History of Halvah," explored its origins as a recipe that appeared in a thirteenth-century Arabic cookbook, where it's treated as a candy more than a dessert. It made its way to Ashkenazi Jews by way of

Economy Candy's original awning; notice how halvah was a featured item. *Mitchell and Skye Cohen, Economy Candy.*

Romania, which was then ruled by the Ottoman empire. Even savvy New Yorkers might not be completely familiar with this very New York treat. In "A Gentile's Guide to Jewish Food," published by *New York Magazine* in 1968, it lists a host of foods such as halvah that were unique to the appetizing store. It described halvah as "beautiful to look at and tastes like a sweet, straw placemat, but good."

Halvah was first produced in America by Nathan Radutzky, who immigrated to New York from the Ukraine in 1907. He lived on the LES, where he made his product in a garage and sold it from a pushcart. He moved his enterprise to Brooklyn, where today the business produces halvah and a variety of chocolate-coated candy. The factory creates the tahini in one factory, and then a pipeline that runs under the street transports it across the street to create the halvah. You might not know the name Radutzky, but you've probably sampled his Joyva products. What began in a small garage on the LES has grown to the largest halvah producer in the country, hence its slogan, "The house that sesame built." The next time you dig into a mound of halvah, one of its chocolate-coated jellied candy rings or marshmallow twists, notice the smiling sultan on Joyva's label, which is a nod to its humble Ottoman beginnings. You can still find a variety of fresh halvah at Economy Candy, along with more than two thousand other sweet treats. Third-generation family members Mitchell and Skye Cohen keep the original feel at Economy Candy. As Skye explained to me, "Being a family owned and operated store (for more than eighty-five years), the friends, neighbors and tourists who shop with us become part of our family when they walk into our shop—which is certainly unique in a city that can be anonymous." You'll need to have more than a penny when you go these days, but you will definitely feel like a kid in a candy store.

~~~

Original New York Cheesecake

(Reprinted with permission from Junior's Cheesecake Cookbook, *Alan Rosen and Beth Allen.)*

9-inch sponge cake crust:

Softened unsalted butter, for buttering the pan
⅓ cup sifted cake flour
¾ teaspoon baking powder
Pinch of table salt
2 extra-large eggs, separated
⅓ cup sugar
1 teaspoon pure vanilla extract
2 drops pure lemon extract
2 tablespoons unsalted butter, melted
¼ teaspoon cream of tartar

1. Preheat the oven to 350°F and generously butter the bottom and sides of a 9- or 8-inch springform pan (preferably a nonstick one). Wrap

the outside with aluminum foil, covering the bottom and extending it all the way up the side.

2. In a small bowl, sift the flour, baking powder and salt together.

3. In a large bowl, using an electric mixer, beat the egg yolks on high for 3 minutes. With the mixer running, slowly add 2 tablespoons of the sugar and continue beating until thick light-yellow ribbons form in the bowl, about 5 minutes more. Beat in the extracts.

4. Sift the flour mixture over the batter and stir it in by hand, just until there are no remaining white flecks. Blend in the melted butter.

5. In another clean bowl, using clean, dry beaters, beat the egg whites and cream of tartar together on high until frothy. Gradually add the remaining sugar and continue beating until stiff peaks form (the whites will stand up and look glossy, not dry). Fold about one-third of the whites into the batter, then the remaining whites. Don't worry if you still see a few white specks, as they'll disappear during baking.

6. Gently spread the batter over the bottom of the prepared pan and bake just until set and golden (not wet or sticky), about 10 minutes. Touch the cake gently in the center. If it springs back, it's done. Watch carefully and don't let the top brown. Leave the crust in the pan and place on a wire rack to cool. Leave the oven on while you prepare the batter for the cheesecake.

For the Batter:

Four 8-ounce packages
cream cheese (use only full fat) at room temperature
1⅔ cups sugar
¼ cup cornstarch
1 tablespoon pure vanilla extract
2 extra-large eggs
¾ cup heavy or whipping cream

Put one package of the cream cheese, ⅓ cup of the sugar and the cornstarch in a large bowl and beat with an electric mixer on low until creamy, about 3 minutes, scraping down the bowl several times. Blend in the remaining cream cheese, one package at a time, scraping down the bowl after each one.

Increase the mixer speed to medium and beat in the remaining 1⅓ cups sugar, then the vanilla. Blend in the eggs, one at a time, beating well

A picture-perfect Junior's cheesecake. *Alan Rosen, Junior's Restaurants.*

after adding each one. Beat in the cream just until completely blended. Be careful not to overmix! Gently spoon the batter over the crust.

Place the cake in a large shallow pan containing hot water that comes about 1 inch up the sides of the springform. Bake until the edges are light golden brown and the top is slightly golden tan, about 1¼ hours. Remove the cheesecake from the water bath, transfer to a wire rack and let cool for 2 hours (just walk away—don't move it). Then, leave the cake in the pan, cover loosely with plastic wrap and refrigerate until completely cold, preferably overnight or for at least 4 hours.

To serve, release and remove the sides of the springform, leaving the cake on the bottom of the pan. Place on a cake plate. Refrigerate until ready to serve. Slice the cold cake with a sharp straight-edge knife, not a serrated one. Cover any leftover cake and refrigerate or wrap and freeze for up to 1 month.

The Junior's Way

Master Baker Michael Goodman said, "Always bake the cheesecake in a water bath, as we do here at Junior's. It keeps the heat in the oven moist and helps the cake bake slowly, gently and evenly. This helps ensure that your cheesecake comes out of the oven with a smooth top—and no large cracks."

~~~

Mini Pistachio Chocolate Halvah Bites

Typically, to enjoy fresh halvah, you'd have to visit an appetizing store, but it's so easy to make at home. These halvah bites are not too anything. They are not too sweet, too chalky or too tahini forward. They are a sublimely sweet nostalgic bite to have with your morning coffee or evening tea.

½ cup confectioner's sugar
½ cup whole milk powder
¼ cup tahini (well stirred)
1 teaspoon pure vanilla extract
¼ cup shelled pistachios, rough chopped
½ cup semi-sweet chocolate chips
24 mini cupcake cups (1.5-inch each)

Homemade bite-sized halvah, great with a cup of tea. *Photo by author.*

In a medium bowl, mix together the sugar and milk powder. Pour in the tahini and stir. Add the vanilla and pistachios and stir to combine. It will resemble clumpy sand.

Turn the mixture out on your counter and knead the dough until it comes together, adding a bit more tahini if the mixture is too dry. The dough should resemble Play-Doh when ready.

Melt the chips in the microwave in 20-second intervals, stirring after each until melted, about 60 seconds.

Line a tray with the mini cups and, using a teaspoon, drop the melted chocolate into the bottom of each cup. Tap the tray on the counter to help evenly distribute the melted chocolate.

Roll the halvah dough into 1-inch balls and lightly press into the cups; if the chocolate comes up the side, no worries—it's a bonus!

Cover and chill 2 hours for soft halvah or 4 hours or overnight for firm. Keep any extra servings in a sealed bag or container in the fridge.

Epilogue

FOOD FOR THOUGHT

*W*e started this journey agreeing to view these iconic foods with a forgiving lens, keeping an open mind about the varied inclusions, celebrating those foods and establishments that have shown remarkable tenacity and remembering those that have faded away. In the end, more than a century after being introduced, the foods that came forward with these brave immigrants managed to change the culinary landscape of New York and, in turn, the food of this nation. After taking this journey, I hope it gave you an appreciation for the ingenuity and perseverance of a group of people who made their mark in creating establishments, trends and industries that spoke volumes about their heritage. I hope you learned a few interesting facts about the origins and provenance of these iconic foods to dazzle your friends and stump your mother-in-law. I hope it whetted your appetite to revisit foods that you might have sworn off—a fatty pastrami sandwich is not going to be your demise. I hope you groaned quietly at the plethora of puns and perhaps added a few of your own that I might have missed. I hope you found humor and insight in the twists of fate and happenstances that moved a cuisine from the streets of New York to mainstream America. If this book was about the people and places that share your lineage, then I hope you found pride in their determination to create a legacy through your ancestral food. If you are new to Jewish cuisine, then I hope you found inspiration to try to re-create these noshes, nibbles and nourishment, bringing new flavors into your home and new traditions to your table. Whether you are a New

From the streets of Orchard and Rivington came many of New York's iconic foods. *NYPL, Irma and Paul Millstein Division of United States History, Local History and Genealogy.*

Yorker by birth, by choice or by airline ticket, I hope you will support the restaurants and businesses that continue to glorify, sanctify and reinvent these iconic foods as if they were a religion. Here's to another century of schmaltz-laden matzo balls, luxuriously silky lox, briny kosher dill pickles and sublimely sweet cheesecake. May your bagels be yeasty, your knishes perfectly golden and your antacids readily at hand.

Opposite: A map depicting the five boroughs that form New York City. *PerryPlanet, Wikimedia Commons.*

WHERE TO GO

*U*sually when someone tells you where to go, they are deriding you, but in this section, I am guiding you to find the foods discussed in the book. All recommendations are based on personal visits, online reviews and in-depth reports from trusted sources. All information was current at the time I drafted the book, but you never know if a store has closed or a restaurant has moved, so please check before heading out. Most of all, be adventurous and go outside your comfort zone and favorite borough (I've listed the borough where each is located to help you plan better). You will be rewarded with New York foods, establishments and experiences that are sure to please. Many of these businesses provide mail order directly or through third party services like Goldbelly. You'll be responsible for creating the appropriate ambience—rude service and kitschy paper hats optional.

Bagel Shops

Absolute Bagels
Manhattan
(212) 932-2052

Bagel Pub
Brooklyn
bagelpub.com

Bagels on the Boulevard
Staten Island
(718) 667-7800
bagelsontheblvd.com

Black Seed Bagels
Brooklyn, Manhattan
blackseedbagels.com

Brooklyn Bagel & Coffee Co
Long Island City, Manhattan
bkbagels.com

Empire Bagels
Bronx
(718) 828-4530
empire-bagels.com

Essa-A-Bagel
Manhattan
(212) 980-1010
ess-a-bagel.com

H&H
Manhattan
hhbagels.com

Kossar's Bagels and Bialys
Manhattan
(212) 473-4810
kossars.com

Leo's Bagels
Manhattan
(212) 785-4700
leosbagels.com

Murray's Bagels
Manhattan
(212) 627-5054
murraysbagels.com

Tompkins Square Bagels
Manhattan
tompkinssquarebagels.com

Utopia Bagels
Queens
(718) 352-2586
utopiabagelsny.com

Appetizing Shops

Barney Greengrass
Manhattan
(212) 724-4707
barneygreengrass.com

Murray's Sturgeon Shop
Manhattan
(212) 724-2650
murrayssturgeon.com

RUSS & DAUGHTERS
Brooklyn, Manhattan
(212) 475-4880
russanddaughters.com

ZABAR'S
Manhattan
(212) 787-2000
zabars.com

SABLES
Manhattan
(212) 249-6177
sablesnyc.com

ZUCKER'S BAGELS AND SMOKED FISH
Manhattan
zuckersbagels.com

SHELSKY'S
Brooklyn
(718) 855-8817
shelskys.com

DELICATESSENS

2ND AVE. (KOSHER)
Manhattan
(212) 689-9000
2ndavedeli.com

LIEBMAN'S DELI (KOSHER)
Bronx (Riverdale)
(718) 548-4534
liebmansdeli.com

BEN'S (KOSHER)
Manhattan, Long Island, Queens
& Florida
bensdeli.net

MILE END
Brooklyn
(718) 852-7510
mileenddeli.com

DAVID'S BRISKET HOUSE
Brooklyn
(718) 789-1155
davidsbriskethouse.com

MILL BASIN DELI (KOSHER)
Brooklyn
(718) 241-4910
millbasindeli.com

FRANKEL'S
Brooklyn
(718) 389-2302
frankelsdelicatessen.com

PASTRAMI QUEEN (KOSHER)
Manhattan
(212) 734-1500
pastramiqueen.com

KATZ'S
Manhattan
(212) 254-2246
katzsdelicatessen.com

SARGES
Manhattan
(212) 679-0442
sargesdeli.com

Pickles

Ba-Tampte
Brooklyn
(718) 251-2100
batamptepickle.com

The Pickle Guys
Manhattan
(212) 656-9739
pickleguys.com

Guss' Pickles
Brooklyn
(718) 933-6060
gusspickle.com

Knish

Gottlieb's Restaurant (Kosher)
Brooklyn
(718) 384-6612
gottliebsrestaurant.com

Yonah Schimmel's Knish (kosher)
Manhattan
(212) 477-2858
knishery.com

Knish Nosh (kosher)
Queens
(718) 897-5554

The Egg Cream

Brooklyn Farmacy & Soda
Fountain
Brooklyn
(718) 522-6260
brooklynfarmacyandsodafountain.
com

Lexington Candy Shop
Manhattan
(212) 288-0057
lexingtoncandyshop.net

Eddie's Sweet Shop
Queens
(718) 520-8514

Peter Pan Donut & Pastry Shop
Brooklyn
(718) 389-3676
peterpandonuts.com

Joe Jr. Restaurant
Manhattan
(212) 473-5150

Ray's Candy Store
Manhattan
(212) 505-7609

SHOPSIN'S
Manhattan
Text (401) 307-3023

TOM'S PROSPECT HEIGHTS
Brooklyn
tomsbrooklyn.com

SWEET TREATS

BREAD'S BAKERY
Manhattan
breadsbakery.com

GREEN'S BAKERY
Brooklyn
(646) 801-8460
greensbabka.com

JUNIOR'S
Manhattan and Brooklyn
juniorscheesecake.com

MICHAELI BAKERY
Manhattan
michaelibakery.com

ORWASHERS
Manhattan, weekends at farmers'
markets throughout the city and
Long Island
orwashers.com

WILLIAM GREENBERG
Manhattan
(212) 861-1340
wmgreenbergdesserts.com

ZARO'S
Locations throughout New York
and New Jersey
zaro.com

EXPERIENCES

There are fabulous food adventures to be discovered throughout the city, with new ones popping up every day. Seek out walking tours, museums, exhibits and all the city has to offer to get the full flavor. Here are a few to get you started.

ACME FISH FRIDAY
Brooklyn
(718) 383-8585
acmesmokedfish.com

Acme Fish opens its smoked fish facilities to the public for a long-standing tradition it calls Fish Friday. This is a chance to buy its world-famous products at wholesale prices. You can call ahead and place your order, all of which are kosher, except smoked sturgeon and smoked tuna salad.

Brooklyn Seltzer Boys
Brooklyn
(718) 649-0800
brooklynseltzerboys.com

Schedule an appointment for a factory tour or to refill/refurbish your seltzer bottle or plan a bubbly off-site event.

Economy Candy
Manhattan
(212) 254-1531
economycandy.com

Bring more than a few pennies to purchase old-time favorites like sugary dots on paper strips and Mallo Cups.

Gefilteria
Brooklyn
(347) 688-8561
gefileria.com

Celebrating eastern European Jewish cuisine (and glorifying gefilte fish) through immersive culinary workshops and collaborative events and projects.

Lox at Café Bergson (Kosher)
Manhattan
(646) 437-4231
loxnewyork.com

This café with a view of the Statue of Liberty and Ellis Island is housed on the second floor of the Museum of Jewish Heritage—a Living Memorial to the Holocaust. Tour the museum and then take time to soak in the lessons over a light bite of Jewish-Russian favorites, including a Jewish bento box or Minsk Matzo Babka.

Nathan's Coney Island Hot Dog
Brooklyn
nathansfamous.com

Despite franchise locations throughout the country, you need to visit where it all began and then stroll the boardwalk at Coney Island, run your toes in the sand or ride one of the coasters (just be sure your hot dog is fully digested well before).

SADELLE'S
Manhattan
(212) 254-3000
sadelles.com

An elegant experience—think champagne and latkes. The pageantry of its signature tower of smoked salmon with thin sliced cucumbers, red onion, tomatoes and capers can be enjoyed with a uniquely spiced salt and pepper bagel in posh surroundings.

2ND FLOOR BAR & ESSEN (KOSHER)
Manhattan
(212) 737-1700
2ndfloor.com

Order a swanky cocktail and dine on bites from pastrami burgers to blintzes stuffed with duck for a Jewish speakeasy experience.

SEED + MILL
Manhattan
seedandmill.com

This is your chance to taste a wide range of halvah and tahini at the famed Chelsea Market.

SHALOM JAPAN
Brooklyn
(718) 388-4012
shalomjapannyc.com

Chefs and owners Aaron Israel and Sawako Okochi team up to create a menu blending their two cultures, including sake Kasu challah or matzo ball ramen.

SHERRY HERRING
Manhattan
(646) 863-2347
sherryherring.com

Reimagining herring and other kosher specialties with an Israeli flair.

SWEET PICKLE BOOKS
Manhattan
sweetpicklebooks.com

Calling itself New York's best pickle bookstore, this kitschy shop on the Lower East Side is where a love of books meets pickle infatuation.

TENEMENT MUSEUM
Manhattan
(877) 975-3786
tenement.org

Travel back in history and explore the challenges and lives of immigrant families.

VESELKA
Manhattan
(212) 228-9682
veselka.com

Since 1964, this Ukrainian New York institution has been serving the best borscht in the city. Enjoy its blintzes, salmon and latke eggs Benedict or famous pierogi.

SELECT BIBLIOGRAPHY

Balinska, Maria. *The Bagel: The Surprising History of a Modest Bread*. New Haven, CT: Yale University Press, 2008.

Bellin, Mildred Grosberg. *The Jewish Cook Book*. New York: Bloch Publishing, 1947.

Brumberg-Kraus, Jonathan. *Gastronomic Judaism as Culinary Midrash*. Lanham, MD: Lexington Books, 2019.

Diner, Hasia. *Hungering for America: Italian, Irish, and Jewish Foodways in the Age of Migration*. Cambridge, MA: Harvard University Press, 2003.

———. *Lower East Side Memories*. Princeton, NJ: Princeton University Press, 2000.

———. *Roads Taken: The Great Jewish Migrations to the New World and the Peddlers Who Forged the Way*. New Haven, CT: Yale University Press, 2018.

———. *A Time for Gathering: The Second Migration, 1820–1880*. Baltimore, MD: Johns Hopkins University Press, 1995.

Frost, Natasha. "The Forgotten History of New York's Bagel Famines: Remembering Local 338 and the World's Toughest Bagel Bakers." Atlas Obscura, February 9, 2018. https://www.atlasobscura.com/articles/bagel-union-strikes-new-york-city.

Goodman, Matthew. "The Rise and Fall of the Bagel." *Harvard Review*, no. 28 (2005).

Hauck-Lawson, Annie, and Jonathan Deutsch. *Gastropolis: Food and New York City*. New York: Columbia University Press, 2008.

Horowitz, Roger. *Kosher USA: How Coke Became Kosher and Other Tales of Modern Food*. New York: Columbia University Press, 2016.

Katchor, Ben. *The Dairy Restaurant*. New York: Nextbook Press, 2020.

Levine, Ed. "Was Life Better When Bagels Were Smaller." *New York Times*, December 31, 2003. https://www.nytimes.com/2003/12/31/dining/was-life-better-when-bagels-were-smaller.html.

Levy, Esther. *Jewish Cookery Book*. Philadelphia, PA: W.S. Turner, 1871. Updated version, Kansas City, MO: Andrews McMeel Publishing, 2012.

Marks, Gil. *The Encyclopedia of Jewish Food*. New York: Houghton Mifflin Harcourt, 2010.

Merwin, Ted. *Pastrami on Rye: An Overstuffed History of the Jewish Deli*. New York: New York University Press, 2015.

Moore, Deborah Dash. *Jewish New York: The Remarkable Story of a City and a People*. New York: New York University Press, 2017.

Rezy, Aaron, and Jordan Schaps. *Eating Delancey: A Celebration of Jewish Food*. Brooklyn, NY: Powerhouse Books, 2014.

Riis, Jacob. *How the Other Half Lives: Studies Among the Tenements of New York*. Reprint, Eastford, CT: Martino Fine Books, 2015.

Rischin, Moses. *The Promised City: New York's Jews, 1870–1914*. Rev. ed. Cambridge, MA: Harvard University Press, 1977.

Roden, Claudia. *The Book of Jewish Food: An Odyssey from Samarkand to New York*. New York: Alfred A. Knopf, 1997.

Rosten, Leo. *The Joys of Yiddish*. New York: McGaw Hill, 1968.

Sax, David. *Save the Deli: In Search of Perfect Pastrami, Crusty Rye, and the Heart of the Jewish Delicatessen*. New York: Houghton Mifflin Harcourt, 2009.

Schwartz, Arthur. *New York City Food: An Opinionated History and More than 100 Legendary Recipes*. New York: Stewart, Tabori & Change, 2004.

Serkin, Rachel. "Pushcarts: The Hustle to the American Dream." Museum at Eldridge Street, December 27, 2016. https://www.eldridgestreet.org/history/pushcarts-the-hustle-to-the-american-dream.

Sheraton, Mimi. *The Bialy Eaters: The Story of a Bread and a Lost World*. New York: September 2000.

Smith, Andrew F. *New York City: A Food Biography*. Lanham, MD: Rowman and Littlefield, 2013.

Sturcken, Charles. "New York City Water Essential Ingredient for Bagel and Pickle Makers at Smithsonian Folklife Festival." City of New York, July 5, 2001. https://www1.nyc.gov/html/dep/html/press_releases/01-27pr.shtml.

Thompson, Helen. "How Chemistry Gives New York City Bagels an Edge." *Smithsonian Magazine* (May 21, 2015). https://www.smithsonianmag.com/smart-news/how-chemistry-gives-new-york-bagels-edge-180955362.

Weinstein, Bernard. *The Jewish Unions in America: Pages of History and Memories*. Translated and annotated by Maurice Wolfthal. Cambridge, UK: Open Book Publishers, 2018.

Wex, Michael. *Rhapsody in Schmaltz: Yiddish Food and Why We Can't Stop Eating It*. New York: St. Martin's Press, 2016.

Ziegelman, Jane. *97 Orchard Street: An Edible History of Five Immigrant Families in One New York Tenement*. New York: Harper Paperbacks, 2011.

ABOUT THE AUTHOR

*J*une Hersh is a cookbook author, speaker and food archivist with a focus on Jewish food. Her bestselling book, *Recipes Remembered: A Celebration of Survival* (Ruder Finn Press, May 2011), is a compendium of stories and recipes gathered from interviews with more than 150 Holocaust survivors. The book, now in its seventh printing, was a charitable endeavor, with all proceeds benefiting the Museum of Jewish Heritage and other Holocaust-related organizations. Subsequent to that, she wrote *The Kosher Carnivore* (St. Martin's Press, September 2011), *Still Here: Inspiration from Survivors and Liberators of the Holocaust* and *Yoghurt: A Global History* (for the Edible Series, published by Reaktion Books). June is currently working on her second book for The History Press focused on the culinary curiosities and contributions of Upstate New York. You can look for it to be released late 2023 or early 2024.

June is a freelance writer for *Westchester Magazine*, contributes regularly to food blogs and is a speaker on the topic of food history and Jewish cooking. She is a proud member of the New York chapter of Les Dames d' Escoffier—she was a contributor for its new cookbook. June lives in Bedford, New York, with her husband and her dog, Mallomar. She enjoys traveling, golfing and, of course, cooking. Her greatest joy is sharing culinary traditions by handing down timeless recipes and family stories to the next generation, to ensure they preserve food memory. Her mantra is "Eat Well—Do Good," which she hopes to accomplish through her books, all of which have a charitable flavor. You can follow her on Instagram and Facebook @junehersh. She welcomes your questions and comments or just to chat via e-mail at junehersh@gmail.com.